Living & Working in
France

Living & Working in
France

*How to prepare for a successful visit,
be it short, long-term, or forever*

ALAN HART

How To Books

Published by How To Books Ltd,
3 Newtec Place, Magdalen Road,
Oxford OX4 1RE. United Kingdom.
Tel: (01865) 793806. Fax: (01865) 248780.
email: info@howtobooks.co.uk
http://www.howtobooks.co.uk

First edition 1998

British Library Cataloguing in Publication Data.
A catalogue record for this book is available from
the British Library.

Cartoons by Mike Flanagan
Cover design by Shireen Nathoo Design
Cover image PhotoDisc

Produced for How To Books by Deer Park Productions
Typeset by PDQ Typesetting, Newcastle-under-Lyme. Staffs.
Printed and bound by Cromwell Press, Trowbridge, Wiltshire

NOTE: The material contained in this book is set out in good
faith for general guidance and no liability can be accepted
for loss or expense incurred as a result of relying in particular
circumstances on statements made in the book. Laws and
regulations are complex and liable to change, and readers should
check the current position with the relevant authorities before
making personal arrangements.

Contents

List of Illustrations

Preface

Upon reflection, it was a strange – but not an ill – wind that first brought me to France. Almost exactly seven years ago, I found out that my plans to spend a year in southern Africa after university were not feasible. Since it had been a long-standing ambition, not surprisingly I was rather 'down', as well as being at a loose end. Shortly afterwards, I was offered the chance to come to Paris for a year, something I would never normally have contemplated. Having dismissed French after O-Levels in favour of German, nothing could have been further from my mind than the idea of a year in the French capital.

Admittedly the first few months were tough, despite being surrounded by a supportive and caring community at St George's Anglican Church in Paris with whom I worked. However, one prediction that was made to me shortly before arriving did come true – that after about three months, I would get the hang of the language, the way of life, and the mentality. From that time onwards, the difficulty was very much in the other direction – coping with the idea of going back to England.

The passage of time has shown what the result was to be! After seven years, four apartments and three jobs, it is my privilege to encourage you to take up a similar sort of challenge. Hopefully, this book will help you do that in a rather more ordered fashion than my own.

What I have tried to do is to provide you with the 'broad outlines' of life and work in France today. Throughout this book, you will find key French words and phrases in bold type. Understanding these will help you to understand what is going on around you during the initial period in France. Obviously it will finally be the particularities of your own lifestyle, and of the region to which you move, which will all add the 'local colour' to my thumb-nail sketch.

Learning the language is crucial to a successful stay of any length in France. Perhaps the most persistent problem that I have noticed all newcomers to France facing is a sense of isolation – cultural, linguistic and personal. I hope very much that this book will help you to overcome the first of those barriers. The second barrier is really up to you. Certainly as your command of French increases, your sense of isolation will diminish.

The final barrier – finding friends, people to whom you can turn not only in times of trouble but also to share happier moments too – is not so very hard to cross either. The British community alone in France numbers about 40,000 people altogether. No matter what your preconception of expatriates might be, you will find in the many English-speaking associations across France a wealth of information, and a rich mix of people, to which you are about to become a welcome addition.

If you are hoping to find a 'never-never' land of endless cocktail parties and easy living – forget it! The majority of English 'expats' today – and those of other nationalities too – are well-integrated and hard-working. However, there is a great deal of fun to be had too, so don't miss out! Do not be shy of contacting the associations mentioned in the Regional Directory at the end of this book. Whilst these associations are commonly misconceived as ghettos of the colonial spirit, in reality you will find that the vast majority of the associations will speed up your integration into French society, as your knowledge and understanding increases.

France has gone through tremendous changes, economically and socially, in the time that I have lived here – and more is on the way. It is an exciting, dynamic country, traditional but innovative, frustrating but enticing. Once you do settle, you may well find, like me, that the French way of life really has got under your skin. Who knows? Perhaps like so many of us you will end up as a 'Rosbif' with 'Frog's Legs' and stay for longer than you expected!

Looking back over the last seven haphazard years, I can only count my blessings that I came to France instead of going to Africa. The reasons for this are all positive. One of the greatest compliments one French friend paid me was to encourage me to stay in France when I was muttering about going back to England. He simply said, 'You can't go back. You belong to us now.' Coming from somebody from Bordeaux, that's quite a compliment! I hope very much that this book will help you to make a similar happy move to France if that is what you wish.

At the same time, friends still sometimes wave their heads at me despairingly and mumble, 'so British' (and proud of it!). There is a lot to be said for a cross-cultural lifestyle. Enjoy the opportunities that such a lifestyle presents, and enjoy learning to see things from a new perspective.

In conclusion, it only remains for me to say, as the French would, '*Soyez le bienvenue, bonne lecture, et bon séjour en France!*

Alan Hart

Acknowledgements

This book has been made possible through the kind co-operation of the following organisations & individuals:

The British Consulates-General in Bordeaux, Lille, Lyon, Marseille and Paris; the Service des Relations Internationales de la Sécurité Sociale (Mme Rivière); the Service ERASMUS at the Sorbonne (Mme Legendre); AGIL (Pascale Rigaud).

Elizabeth Bernsaconi, Joan Boyer, Judith Boschet, Jean-Luc Brian, Christopher Chantrey, Peggy and Walter Emerson, Paul Hardman, Christophe and Jenny Mailhé, Paddy Salmon. Thanks are also due to Nikki Read and the 'How To' team for their patience in dealing with a working author.

Special thanks are due to Barbara and Julian Aveling not only for the help and information they supplied, but also for all help and support they have given to the author throughout his time in France. If you are lucky enough to find friends such as these during your time in France, it will definitely be a successful stay.

This book is dedicated with affection to Fr Martin Draper and the congregation past and present of St George's Anglican Church in Paris who first brought me to live in France.

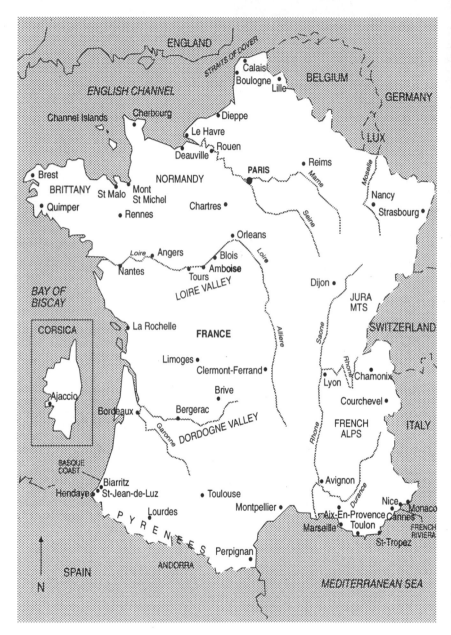

Fig. 1. Map of France.

1
Introducing France

OVERVIEW: THE GEOGRAPHY OF FRANCE

France, which covers 549,000 square kilometres, is the largest country in western Europe. It is a land of climatic and geographical contrasts, and enclosed by the mountainous ski-slopes of the Alps and the Pyrenees lie the verdant pastures of the Ile de France and Limousin: the vineyards, most notably of the Loire valley and the area around Bordeaux; the remote hills and rugged plateaux of the Auvergne; the industrialised landscapes of the north; and the sophisticated, cosmopolitan resorts of the Mediterranean south.

The five principal rivers are the Seine (which flows through Paris), the Loire and the Rhône (along which grow many fine vines), the Garonne in the west, and the Rhine in the east which forms a natural border with France's old enemy and new trade and political partner, Germany. In addition a lattice of canals, soon to be crowned by a Rhine–Rhône Canal 140 miles in length, completes a superb transport network which accounts for 40 per cent of all the waterways of Europe.

North and north-western France (Brittany, Normandy, Picardy, the Ile de France) generally enjoy a 'British' climate of milder winters and pleasant summers. Eastern and central France (Alsace, the Vosges, the Rhône valley, Burgundy, the Auvergne) generally have colder winters with heavier snow, and more clearly defined seasons. In the south and south-west (Provence, the Midi, Aquitaine, the Basque country) winters are occasionally cold but summers are almost invariably – sometimes tropically – hot, from Nice in the east to Biarritz in the west.

GETTING TO KNOW THE PEOPLE

Town and country

The total population of France in 1997 was 58.4 million. The vast majority of the population is concentrated in the industrialised regions of northern and eastern France and the Rhône valley. Public concern over the continuing 'desertification' of certain areas of rural France is matched by regular government subsidies to the traditional industries of farming and fishing which are still treated with great reverence.

Nonetheless France's real wealth now lies in the newer high-technology industries. These are to be found in and around Paris, which dominates France economically (the population of the greater Paris region is approximately 10 million), and around the other major cities and ports of Lyon, Marseille, Lille, Bordeaux and Toulouse. Not unnaturally it is to these major cities that the greatest population drift has taken place from the rural communities. Paris in particular is very much a 'city of exiles', with a low number of born-and-bred Parisians.

Whilst the cities most naturally draw young single people to study and work in them, many French people return frequently to the countryside either to their family homes or to their newly acquired holiday homes. The Friday evening rush hour departure from Paris in particular to the nearby regions of Normandy, the Loire Valley and Burgundy is best avoided!

Origins

As is evidenced by the diversity of languages, cultures and names, the French have experienced several waves of immigration over the centuries. Roman Gaul was conquered eventually by Clovis who was baptised as the first Christian king of 'France' in 496 AD by St Rémy. In 1996 the 1500th anniversary of this baptism, claimed by some as a means of celebrating France's Catholic heritage and reviled by others in the name of the secular state born of the Revolution, provoked a fierce debate during the Papal visit.

Several centuries later Charlemagne's Holy Roman Empire based on France splintered under his divided offspring, and left the kings of France in reality only as kings of the Ile de France until the end of the fifteenth century.

The independent kingdoms and duchies of Brittany, Burgundy, the Languedoc and Provence, and the disputed territories of the Loire Valley and the south west which provoked the Hundred Years War with England, all developed their own cultural identities and in some cases their own languages. These are still important today, most notably in Brittany, the Basque and Catalan regions bordering Spain, the island of Corsica, Provence, and in the oft-disputed Germanic region of Alsace-Lorraine which even has some laws unique to the region.

Immigrations

Strong regional accents are to be found throughout France, some of which can be difficult even for native French speakers to understand! In the south the influence of Italian and Spanish immigrants is strong. This Mediterranean influence has been added to over the years by Portuguese immigrants, mainly to be found in the industrial centres. Between the two world wars, nearly three million immigrants came to France, mainly of Slavic origins – White Russians fleeing the Revolution, and Poles in particular.

More recently immigrants have arrived from France's former colonies in Africa, most notably the **maghreb** countries of Algeria, Morocco and Tunisia. Together with the former French colonials (or **pieds noirs** – literally 'black feet'), this has been a very significant immigration, and France now has over three million Muslim residents principally of African origin. In addition, as with previous immigrations, there have been distinct effects with the development of a dialect and culture, mainly to be found in the large city suburbs, combining north African and French influences.

Finally, there is also a large and thriving British community not only in Paris, but also in Provence and the Dordogne, and scattered throughout the country. Recent estimates place the size of the community at about 40,000 people, mainly concentrated in the Ile de France.

UNDERSTANDING MANNERS AND VALUES

The 'average' French person

An 'average' person is no easier to find in France than anywhere else in the world. Generally the French are conservative, with a strong, almost nostalgic, belief in the 'traditional' values of family, home, and a protective and generous welfare state.

They are a highly individualistic people, who tend to shy away from organised activities and to concern themselves with their own personal situations. (The French describe this attitude by the phrase, *Chacun défend son bifsteack* – roughly translated as 'everybody looks after his affairs'.) This individualism probably goes a long way towards explaining the constant splintering of political parties and trade unions, and perhaps also the latent but still evident hostility to European union.

Negative aspects of the French character which often strike foreigners are intolerance, particularly of non-French methods and modes of thinking: patriotism which at times appears to verge on

xenophobia; and condescension towards foreigners. Criticism and
complaining are national pastimes from which nobody and nothing
is exempt.

However, the many positive traits to the French character should
also be remembered. The great French senses of passion for the
causes they defend, and of style for which they are renowned, are
matched also by a clear appreciation of intelligence and talent in all
its forms. Philosophy is a compulsory school subject in France, and
the country of Pascal, Descartes and Voltaire is still deeply
influenced by their thoughts and those of their successors.
National problems almost inevitably are the subject of a great
debate in the media, with each side producing a philosopher to back
their cause.

In conclusion, whilst the French can appear to be haughty, they
are in fact very welcoming to foreigners who try and communicate
with them in their own language.

Formality and courtesy

Good manners are universally appreciated. In France, formality in
speech and conduct is very prevalent. From the earliest age the
French are taught to address adults as **Monsieur**, **Madame** or
Mademoiselle. The latter form of address should be reserved for
young ladies. Be careful that you do not unintentionally cause offence
by misusing the term Mademoiselle. Even when you know full well
that a lady is a spinster, she ought to be addressed as Madame. To
address her as Mademoiselle is to imply that she is an 'old maid'!
Neighbours may well remain Monsieur or Madame forever.

Unless you have been specifically introduced to a French person
by their first name, avoid using that name until invited to do so.
What is considered friendliness elsewhere will be considered over-
familiarity in France, and will be dealt with accordingly!

Another cardinal rule of courtesy in France is the use of **tu** and
vous. French people will let you know when they are ready to be 'tu-
toied'. Otherwise, you should stick to using the more formal **vous**
form of address. Using **tu** implies an intimacy which is mainly
inappropriate. Foreigners are often forgiven this fault on the grounds
of ignorance. Demonstrating that you understand and can apply the
rule will considerably enhance your standing with French people.

A basic gesture you will see all day and everywhere is the shaking
of hands when people meet, and again when they say goodbye.
Ladies may offer their cheeks to close friends for the **bises** (more
properly the **bisous**). How many kisses (or pecks on the cheek) are

exchanged depends once again on intimacy, and even geographical location – Parisians often give two on each cheek, whilst provincials only give one on each cheek. Once again, stick to the formal hand-shake until you are invited to use this form of greeting.

Many of these rules are universal, although amongst younger people in their twenties and under, the rules are much less hard-and-fast. Cheeks are offered more freely, and **tu** is an acceptable form of address. But where their social etiquette is concerned, let the French guide you until you are confident that you know the rules of the game. Showing you know how to behave 'properly' will paradoxically often lead more quickly to a relaxed atmosphere and relationship.

Privacy

In general, the French are a very private people who do not wish to reveal more about themselves than is necessary. Personal questions about family, lifestyle or business are often avoided or rebuffed. The Anglo-Saxon obsession with the private lives of the rich and famous, as well as the next-door neighbours, is a source of amusement to the French. Private lives are considered to be just that, and lifestyles and relationships are not considered topics of public discussion as in Great Britain or the USA.

Religion

Just as in England most people are nominally 'Church of England', so in France most people are nominally Roman Catholic. In spite of the Revolution of 1789, and the separation of Church and State in 1905, the Catholic inheritance is still strong. However, Mass attendance is on average low (about 14 per cent nationally), and one priest more often than not serves several villages.

About 2 per cent of the population are Protestant, included amongst which are the Anglicans in France with almost thirty chaplaincies across the country. About another 2 per cent of the population are Jewish, and they have produced many distinguished writers and politicians.

Finally there are over three million Muslims in France, mainly immigrants of north African origin. The strains that are placed upon French Muslims with divided loyalties between Islamic law and western culture have led to a number of clashes both within the French Muslim community (especially over the conduct and dress of French Muslim women), and in society as a whole with Algerian Islamic extremism gaining significant footholds amongst the alienated younger Islamic communities of the poorer city suburbs.

The later 1990s has also seen an increased interest in the activity of cults in France, which whilst they remain insignificant numerically, have been a cause for serious concern. A Parliamentary commission is now reviewing laws governing cults.

Social values

Marriage is still the bedrock of French society, although **unions libres** (common-law marriages) are increasingly widespread. Family life is supported and encouraged by generous benefits (**allocation familiale**), schools equipment benefits, tax breaks and reduced transport costs for large families.

The new Socialist government has promised to introduce a **Pacte d'Intérêt Commun (PIC)** (also known as the **Contrat d'Union Sociale or CUS**) which will include equal rights for same-sex couples as for those in **unions libres**. It should be noted that alternative lifestyles other than traditional marriage and family life are sometimes less well-received outside Paris.

The decline of traditional marriage and family patterns is one area where French society is in flux. For generations, compulsory military service for young men has been another pillar of French society. The abolition of military service for those born after June 1979 has opened a new as yet undefined chapter in French society.

The ten-month military service is to be replaced by a still undefined – and fiercely debated – 'Citizens' Encounter (**Rencontre Citoyenne**) of anything from one to three days for all young people aged eighteen, at which they will be encouraged to undertake voluntary work and develop their 'citizen skills'. Quite how this is going to work is unclear, and has yet to be debated in the French Parliament.

Finally, Anglo-Saxon women may well find France a great deal more sexist than either the United Kingdom or the USA. Whilst women have made significant advances in business and have always been prominent in the arts, Anglo-Saxon women still sense a great deal of chauvinism in the attitudes shown to them.

The new Prime Minister Lionel Jospin has followed the British lead in naming three women – Martine Aubry, Elisabeth Guigou and Dominique Voynet – as three of his most senior ministers in an effort to lead the way in establishing greater equality.

UNDERSTANDING THE POLITICAL LIFE

Rulers and republics since 1789

Since their first revolution in 1789, the French have been ruled by a number of kings, consuls, emperors and presidents in succession. The First Republican rulers (1792–95) were replaced by the Directory (**Directoire**), who in turn gave way rapidly to the forceful character of the First Consul, military genius and from 1804 to 1814 the first Emperor of the French, Napoleon. Napoleon was not simply a great general, but also a great law-giver, and the codification of French law is still largely based upon his Code Napoléon laid down in this period.

After his final defeat in 1815 at the battle of Waterloo, Napoleon was replaced by the restored Bourbon monarchy under Louis XVIII (1815–24) and his reactionary brother Charles X (1824–30), the younger brothers of the beheaded Louis XVI. July 1830 saw another revolution in France, less bloody than its predecessor. The life of Charles X was spared, but his throne was lost to his more egalitarian cousin Louis-Philippe (whose father Philippe, Duc d'Orléans, known as Philippe Egalité, voted to execute his cousin Louis XVI!).

Louis-Philippe adopted a more restrained and deliberately *bourgeois* style of monarchy, which lasted until 1848 when revolutions swept across Europe toppling monarchs in their wake. Hence France went through her third revolution in less than fifty years.

A Second Republic was established, under the nephew of the first emperor. Unsurprisingly, this second Bonaparte could not resist following family tradition, and had himself declared Emperor of the French as Napoleon III in 1851. Unlike his uncle, Napoleon III was a great Anglophile, and it was indeed to England that he fled when he was overthrown by the Commune in 1870 after the Franco-Prussian War. During his reign, many of the foundations were laid of Franco-British rapprochement which came to fruition in the *Entente Cordiale* in 1907.

The Third Republic which was eventually established in 1875 lasted until 1940, when France capitulated to the invading Nazi forces and was divided into the occupied territories of the north, and the southern régime of Marshal Pétain based at Vichy which eventually came under Nazi control. Following the liberation of France and the end of the Second World War, a Fourth Republic was established, lasting from 1946 to 1958.

The new Fifth Republic adopted by referendum in 1958 was inspired by the ideas of General Charles de Gaulle, the French wartime resistance leader, who went on to become President (1958–69) and whose spirit still dominates French right-wing politics.

Increased presidential power and a reduced capacity for the **Assemblée Nationale** (Parliament) to bring down the government were built into the new constitution to try and eradicate the political instability of the Third and Fourth Republics.

De Gaulle was succeeded as President by Georges Pompidou, who opened the way to British entry to the Common Market before his death in 1974. He was succeeded by Valérie Giscard d'Estaing who beat François Mitterand to the presidency in 1974. In 1981, however, Mitterand's historic fourteen-year reign began as the first Socialist President of the Fifth Republic. His style of leadership inspired a confidence which allowed him to survive many crises, and which earned him the affectionate nick-names of both '**Ton-ton**' (uncle) and quite simply '**Dieu**' (God).

'La Fracture Sociale' – France in transition
Jacques Chirac's election as President of France in 1995 was a close-won victory which reflected the divided state of France. The reins of government were already divided in a **Cohabitation** between the Socialist President François Mitterand and his right-wing Prime Minster Edouard Balladur. The presidential election gave Chirac a slim majority, and the tables were turned in 1997 with the election of his Socialist challenger in the presidential elections, Lionel Jospin, as the new Prime Minister.

For the third time in fifteen years the principal of 'divide and rule' has been chosen by the French people to provide political checks and balances to the head of state, with a government formed from those in opposition to the elected president. Alain Juppé's ousted right-wing régime (1995–7) had begun the path to British-style economic liberalism, and state-owned industries were prepared for privatisation in order to raise funds for both France's enormous social security debt, and the financial criteria of the Maastricht Agreement for European Monetary Union (EMU). Cuts in public spending and record unemployment (12.5 per cent) led to an almost general and very bitter strike by public-sector workers in the winter of 1995. To a large extent this was the manifestation of the France of divided ideologies which had already duelled in the summer presidential elections.

The race to beat the Maastricht clock and qualify for entry to the EMU has also aggravated old political wounds over France's role in the new Europe. The presidential elections of 1995 saw the extreme-right anti-European parties gain a total of 20 per cent of the vote in the first-round elections. These same parties also advocated a far more draconian anti-immigration policy, which in turn has added to the sense of exclusion many young French citizens of immigrant origins have felt. This is also due to the strict but almost unworkable immigration laws introduced by Charles Pasqua, Minister of the Interior under Edouard Balladur, and his successor Jean-Louis Debré.

The north African communities in particular are concentrated in the poorer suburbs and cités (high-rise dwellings) constructed in the 1970s seemingly to keep them 'out of sight and out of mind'. Both unemployment and crime are high in the cités, and youth unemployment has been named as one of the major priorities by both President Chirac and Prime Minister Jospin.

More widely, attempts are being made to combat the sense of exclusion these young people feel, and concrete expressions of solidarité are promised. The great challenge for the new Socialist government now is to find a compassionate way to balance the books, both creating jobs and safeguarding the present benefits system whilst bringing the financial crisis under control.

The roles of the President and the Prime Minister

The French system of government is a combination of presidential and parliamentary systems.

The President of the Republic

Under the new régime of cohabitation major policy decisions on defence and foreign policy remain the reserve of the President, who is Head of State and Commander-in-Chief of the Armed Forces. He appoints the Prime Minster, presides over the Cabinet and concludes treaties. He may submit questions to the French Parliament by a national referendum, and he may dissolve the Assemblée Nationale, the lower house of the French Parliament.

He is elected by direct universal suffrage for a term of seven years. Elections normally take place in two rounds, which lead to political realignments between each ballot (scrutin) as the leading right-wing and left-wing candidates draw together their forces.

The Prime Minister

The head of the government is the Prime Minister, who heads the Cabinet. He submits government bills to the Parliament and is responsible for their implementation once they have been voted into law.

The French Parliament

The French Parliament is bi-cameral, that is, it has two chambers as in most democracies.

* The 'lower house', the **Assemblée Nationale** (National Assembly) is the more important of the two houses. It may initiate laws, overrule the Sénat, and by a 'motion of censure' force a government to resign. The 491 **Députés** (members) of the Assemblée are elected for a five-year term by a two-round majority vote. To be elected on the first ballot, a candidate must obtain an absolute majority (rare in France) of the valid votes cast, i.e. more than 50 per cent of the votes. If no candidates meet this requirement, a second ballot takes place the following Sunday for candidates who have received at least 12.5 per cent of the votes in the first round. As with the presidential elections, realignments and redistribution of votes between the two ballots are crucial to a candidate's success or failure.

* The **Sénat** (Senate) is the second elected body, made up of 283 Senators, indirectly elected for nine years by an electoral college. Distinguished former Députés and ministers often move up to the Sénat in order to continue in political life but in a reduced capacity.

Political parties

In the spring of 1997, President Jacques Chirac took a political gamble which did not pay off, when he chose to dissolve a year earlier than was necessary the existing Assemblée Nationale, where the ruling right-wing coalition which he headed had a majority. Deep unpopularity at the austerity measures and plans for the liberalisation of the French economy led to a massive swing to the left, and Lionel Jospin now heads a mainly Socialist left-wing coalition government, which is nonetheless dependent on the Communist and Green parties for support in the Assemblée Nationale. Thus France has re-entered once again the state of **cohabitation** between right-wing and left-wing political parties.

The resounding defeat of the right-wing parties has led to a change of leadership and of style, which follows on directly from similar changes in the Socialist leadership a few years ago. Both the right-wing RPR and the left-wing Socialists have in recent years been involved in serious corruption and party funding scandals, and so change was almost inevitable. Following the continued rise in the influence of the Front National in 1998, President Chirac has now initiated a 'review' of French political life.

Socialist Party

The **Socialist Party** or **PS** is currently led by Lionel Jospin. The guiding lights of his new reformed post-Mitterand party are Jacques Delors (the former European Commissioner), Martine Aubry (Delors' daughter) and Dominique Strauss-Kahn (the Finance minister). Traditionally strong in the north of France and the Bouches du Rhône district, in 1997 the Socialists drew widespread support across France, and made significant inroads in traditionally right-wing Paris where they ousted one leading government minister. This position was further strengthened in the regional elections in March 1998. The Socialist programme is built on the following principles:

● Improvement of the working conditions of the labour force. This includes reducing the working week to 35 hours, paid at the rate of 39 hours per week.

● Active governmental role in the economy through nationalised industries. This does not, however, now seem to exclude some limited measure of 'privatisation' or share flotation in state-owned companies.

● Commitment to European Union. However, this is qualified by a desire to establish a 'social Europe' of improved workers' rights.

● Commitments to resolving the problem of youth unemployment, and to safeguarding state benefits.

● Working alliance with the Communist and Green parties, and a number of other smaller left-wing parties.

Right-wing parties

The **Rassemblement for the Republic** or **RPR** has had a chequered history in recent years. The successor to General de Gaulle's political movement, its leader is President Jacques Chirac. Following his defeat in the 1997 elections, former Prime Minister Alain Juppé stepped down from the leadership role he had assumed following Chirac's election, to make way for the more centrist figure of Philippe Seguin, formerly President of the Assemblée Nationale.

The party suffered badly in the 1997 elections, and once again in the 1998 regional elections, and several ministers were ousted from their seats. Splits between the more moderate followers of Seguin, and the more right-wing followers of former Prime Minister Edouard Balladur and the hard-line former Interior Minister

Charles Pasqua, have been almost forgotten, as new divides have opened up between those prepared to collaborate with the Front National and those who refuse all dialogue following the regional elections of Spring 1998.

The RPR programme is built upon the following principles:

• Total opposition to both Communism on the one hand, and the Front National on the other.

• Massive investment in, and liberalisation of, the economy, with increased consumer spending power leading to economic regeneration.

• Commitment to European Union, and to meeting the financial requirements for entry to EMU.

• A new commitment to resolving the problems of mass unemployment and safeguarding the French welfare state, whilst reducing the government deficit (the 'social right' or **droit social**).

• A more stringent application of the immigration laws to cut both legal and illegal immigration.

The **Union for French Democracy** or **UDF** was the other partner in the 1995–97 right-wing government. A fragile coalition of five centre-right parties, the UDF faces an uncertain future after the 1998 elections. For the moment the party remains under the leadership of former Defence Minister François Leotard. The party has a political basis much akin to the RPR with whom they frequently cooperate.

Former Finance Minister and Thatcherite admirer Alain Madelin has now split away from the UDF, although his **Democratie Libérale** party is still closer to the UDF and RPR than to any other groups. Madelin has made clear that he intends to fight for a greatly increased liberalisation of the French economy and an end to restrictive French employment practices. As such, he has made himself the chief enemy of the left-wing trade unions.

Other parties
The **Communist Party** or **PC** led by Robert Hue continues to have a stable if small base of support in France (about 10 per cent in the 1997 elections). Overall their Communism is 'Leninist'. The newspaper *l'Humanité* is their official mouthpiece, and they control the largest and most powerful union, the CGT.

The **Green Party (les Verts)** led by Dominique Voynet also increased their electoral support in 1997. Lionel Jospin's cabinet now includes two green Party members, including Voynet as Minster of the Environment, as well as Communist members.

Finally the 1990s has seen the rise of extreme-right political parties in France. Philippe de Villiers' **Mouvement pour la France** represents about 5 per cent of the electorate, taking a strong Catholic moral stance and a firmly anti-European line.

Much more sinister is the rise of the **Front National** led by Jean-Marie Le Pen and Bruno Maigret, which emerged in 1981 and in 1995 gained 15 per cent of votes cast in the presidential elections. Le Pen's demagogic style mixes tough anti-immigration talk, blaming immigrants for France's unemployment and advocating repatriation, with a sweeping invective against President Chirac and the RPR for their support for European Union.

Le Pen's rallying cry is 'The French first', and he makes free and easy use of French history to support his ideas. Many protest voters are drawn to the Front National, who now control three local councils in the south of France. In Spring 1998 the Front National once again took nearly 16 per cent of the votes in the regional elections, leaving them as power-brokers in many regions. This has led to mayhem in French right-wing politics.

Local government

France is divided into 96 **départements** each managed by a Prefect appointed by the central government, and 36,000 **communes** led by **maires** (mayors) who are agents both of central government and the municipalities. These two tiers form the backbone of an administrative system established by Napoleon I to rule the country under the watchful eye of central government.

However, since 1972 continued efforts have been made to decentralise that system in favour of elected local authorities. In that year, 22 regions were created by grouping together several départements at a time. This was intended to bring local government more under the control of local people. Additional reforms ten years later, in 1982, further decentralised decision-making powers to regional councils, general councils in the départements, and municipal councils in the communes.

UNDERSTANDING THE ECONOMIC LIFE

With the 'silicon valley' of Sophia Antipolis on the south coast, the Aerospace industry in Toulouse, the industries of Lyon and the Rhône valley, and nuclear industry sites across France, the French

have successfully pursued a decentralisation policy away from Paris
which nonetheless continues to dominate the country.

The economic crisis of the 1990s hit France in the same way as
Great Britain, but at a later stage. By the end of 1996, unemployment
in France was at a record 12.5 per cent despite the best efforts of the
right-wing Juppé government to curb state spending, encourage
foreign investors and increase public spending power.

Privatisation and European Monetary Union (EMU)

The need to meet the criteria for entry to the European Monetary
Union (EMU) – a public deficit of no more than 3 per cent of Gross
Domestic Product – and a huge social security debt, saw the Juppé
government (1995–97) accelerating the programme of privatisations
begun under Edouard Balladur.

The new Socialist Jospin government has confirmed that it intends
to continue the privatisation programme on the grounds of 'needs
must', in order to ensure France's entry to EMU in 1999. Whilst
EMU is held responsible for many of the current miseries of the
French people, one group at least is eagerly awaiting France's entry to
the system. These are the brokers at the hitherto relatively insignificant
Paris Stock Exchange (**Bourse**), who like their counterparts in
Frankfurt hope to successfully challenge the dominance of London
in financial markets as the British equivocate over entering EMU.

The announcement that the Jospin government intends to pursue
the privatisation programme of its right-wing predecessor on a 'case
by case' basis will no doubt provoke conflict with the trade unions
and disappointment with a number of electors. 'The idea of
privatisation has been totally incompatible for decades with the
pronouncements of the French left,' wrote Pascal Riché in the left-
wing newspaper *Libération* (19 July 1997). However, the same article
went on to quote an opinion poll conducted in May 1997 during the
parliamentary elections which showed that, 'the Socialists' refusal to
privatise the large publicly-owned companies such as Air France,
France Télécom or Thomson was judged unrealistic by the French
(51 per cent against 43 per cent).' Times have certainly changed in
France, and this is no longer the state of nationalised industries, but
of industries with determinant government shareholdings.

Foreign investment

Since 1994 there has been a remarkable opening-up of the
previously protected French markets, partly due to a more liberal
internal economic policy and partly due to European directives

from Brussels. In 1996, the largest foreign investment in France was British valued at US$15.4 billion. American investors came next ($12.65 billion), followed by the Swiss ($4.26 billion), the Germans ($3.5 billion) and the Italians ($3.48 billion).

The banking sector has been faced with a crisis resulting from heavy over-investment in the so-called 'safe' property market. Together with the insurance sector, there has been major restructuring in private banks and insurance companies, as well as in former state-owned companies. Much of this has been due to foreign investment. The troubled state-controlled banks Crédit Lyonnais and Crédit Foncier de France (the specialist property bank) both reported spectacular losses, and government bail-outs have been necessary in both cases. These have met with fierce opposition from the private sector, and close scrutiny from Eurocrats in Brussels.

Not all foreign investors and their ideas are welcome in France. The Korean firm Daewoo – already well-implanted in France – have provoked hostile reactions due to work practices. DHL have failed twice to find a site in eastern France willing to accept a busy night-time airport. Both companies have offered substantial job creation, but neither are welcomed by a conservative population who value standards of living.

Several imminent restructuring programmes (**plans socials**) have caused deep unease. They are seen as part of a globalisation (**mondialisation**) of the economy, from which France has been spared due to the lack of previous internationalisation in French companies and ownership, and closed markets. High social charges remain an obstacle to expansion for many companies.

Anglo-French trade

Trade figures for 1996 showed impressive Franco-British activity. France was the UK's third largest market, taking 10.2 per cent of total UK exports, and overall the UK was France's fourth largest supplier. France meanwhile was the UK's third largest supplier, providing 9.6 per cent of total imports.

Whilst the British were busy buying up or into French companies in 1996, a reverse process was taking place on the other side of the Channel. With the sale of British utilities, French companies have cashed in on opportunities to expand internationally. In 1996, French direct investment in the UK amounted to FF5.9 bn, representing 4.3 per cent of total French direct investment world-wide.

The new Anglophilia which has grown up since about 1994 has been largely inspired by the success of the Channel Tunnel and the

Eurostar service linking London and Paris. Some French companies have now begun to invest in Kent (only two hours by train from Lille) in order to take advantage of more liberal British employment laws and lower social charges.

Ironically the symbol of this new *Entente Cordiale*, Eurotunnel, is the most troubled of all Franco-British ventures. Following the fire in the tunnel in 1996, shareholders will not now receive a dividend until 2006. Several restructuring plans have had to be devised to satisfy the banks who largely financed the original project. Nevertheless, there is already talk of building a second tunnel under the Channel. Meanwhile the ferry companies and airlines are locked in a bitter price war with Eurotunnel to try and retain their custom. Once again, this has led to new alliances.

The role and power of the unions

French unions are numerous but are neither as highly organised nor as powerful as those of her main economic rivals. Union membership, at about 20 per cent, is amongst the lowest in Europe. The power of the unions, however, comes from their strongholds in the public sector, particularly transport, which enables them to cripple the economy rapidly and at will. Strikes are called regularly, and the situation is most reminiscent of that in Great Britain before the reforms at the beginning of the 1980s under Margaret Thatcher.

A local branch (**section syndicale**) of a Union can be established in any company with at least 50 employees. Union negotiations are carried out at national or regional level between major employers' associations and labour organisations (not all are trade unions). Resulting agreements are then applied throughout that particular industry. In some cases, there may well be 'knock-on' effects in other industries where workers will claim the same rights.

Labour relations are based on a contractual policy (**politique contractuelle**) introduced since the riots of 1968. This provides for renewable and therefore renegotiable labour contracts. This type of collective bargaining not only includes working conditions but also retirement, training, the indexation of wages and prices, and job security.

The main unions

The leading union federations are fragmented and divided along political lines. Most unions are either run by or closely related to political parties. To a very large extent the unions consider themselves to be 'the Fourth Estate' politically, and to have the right to issue political demands – ultimately backed by strike action – to any government.

- The **Conféderation Générale du Travail (CGT)**. This is the largest and most belligerent union. The leaders are Communist or Communist-affiliated and controlled. They are geographically strongest in the heavy industrialised regions around Paris and Marseilles, and in heavy industry, metallurgy, mining, ports, electricity and railways.

- The **Conféderation Française Démocratique du Travail (CFDT)** is the most organised and active of the non-Communist unions. Its members are mostly white-collar workers in the metallurgical, gas and chemical industries.

- The **Force Ouvrière (FO)** is more moderate in tone than the CGT but normally co-operates with the CGT and other left-wing unions in major 'policy' matters. It is the leading federation of workers in the nationalised industries and the civil service. Its strongholds are Paris and the south-west.

- The **Conféderation Français des Travailleurs Chrétiens (CFTC)**, founded in 1919, is a federation of miners and certain white-collar workers in mining, banking, insurance, air traffic control, the oil industry, glass and ceramics. It is found country-wide.

- The **Conseil National du Patronat Français (CNPF)** represents employers in their relations with the government and decides to some extent the employers' economic and social policy. Membership is drawn from banking, business and industry country-wide.

The principal unions (CGT, FO, CFDT) are primarily but not exclusively concerned with workers in the nationalised industries. As such they are vociferous in their opposition to privatisation, and in defence of their **acquis sociaux** (basically this means 'perks').

All the unions are strong advocates of the reduction of the working week from 39 to 35 hours per week, paid at the rate of 39 hours. They claim that this will create jobs, and are supported in this call by the Communist Party. The introduction of this fiercely debated policy is planned for the year 2000.

Unrest and protest

It seems that scarcely a day goes by without some form of strike (**grève** – sometimes also called a **mouvement social**), protest, demonstration (**manifestation** or **manif'** for short), one-day stoppage or embargo taking place in France. Cynics have commented that ever since 1789, it has been mob rule that has prevailed in France. A quick glance at the country's history – the Revolutions of 1830 and 1848, the Commune of 1870, and the disturbances of 1968 – suggests that there might actually be some truth in that jibe.

In 1995 government employees led a hard three-month strike in protest at government attempts to suppress posts in the extensive civil service. In 1996, lorry drivers blockaded France, paralysed her food supplies, and wreaked international financial havoc whilst the police observed from the sidelines. In the same year, angry employees at the state-controlled bank Crédit Foncier de France took their director 'hostage' for a week. Farmers regularly dump large quantities of unsaleable produce on the doorsteps of government buildings, and attack foreign convoys of goods. Cattle farmers hit by the BSE crisis marched their herds across France and up to the Eiffel Tower before demanding – and receiving – an interview with President Chirac.

Generally the unwritten French commandment seems to be 'Strike, and thou shalt receive.' However, the French generally prefer to regard such behaviour as another form of the liberty of expression.

UNDERSTANDING THE LEGAL SYSTEM

Britain is a **common law** country in which the system of justice depends heavily on custom and precedent. However, France is a **civil law** country where the legal system is based entirely on a body of written law.

A system of **administrative justice** was laid down by Napoleon I in the **Code Napoléon** (Napoleonic Code), which was later also adopted by other countries. Today there are 55 'codes' (compilations of laws, decrees and circulars) governing all branches of French law. Amongst these are the **Code Civil**, the **Code Pénal**, and the **Code Fiscal**.

In France there are actually two judicial systems: administrative and judiciary. The administrative system is responsible for settling lawsuits between the government and the individual. This provides French citizens with exceptional legal protection. Suits are brought to the 22 **Tribunaux de Première Instance** and appeals may be made to the **Conseil d'Etat** (Council of State). This is one of the most prestigious bodies in France. One of its roles is to advise the government on the conformity of proposed legislation with the body of existing law.

Running parallel to the administrative system is the **judiciary** which is responsible for civil and criminal cases. The criminal courts include the **Tribunaux correctionels** (Courts of Correction), the **Tribunaux de police** (Police Courts), and the **Cours d'assises** (Assize Courts), which try felonies. Appeals are referred to one of the 28 **Cours d'appel** (Courts of Appeal).

All court decisions are subject to possible reversal by the Supreme Court of Appeals (the **Cour de Cassation**). All judges in France are career professionals who must pass a very competitive examination. In criminal courts the judge has a more active role in the case than in Great Britain and conducts most of the questioning of the witness. A French jury is actually a mixed tribunal where six lay judges sit with three professional judges. A two-thirds majority of this 'jury' may convict. The jury of peers (as used in Great Britain) was abolished in 1941 in France.

In January 1997 President Chirac established a commission to propose reforms to the French legal system. There has traditionally been a strong link between the government and investigating magistrates, which has led to political pressure being exerted in sensitive cases relating to government affairs and public figures. Reforms are now expected to break these links and provide magistrates and judges with a freer hand to tackle political corruption.

UNDERSTANDING THE EDUCATION SYSTEM

The excellent French education system is highly competitive throughout, freely available and uniformly under state control from nursery school through to sixth form level. After the riots of 1968 which began as student disturbances, education was one area in which values were re-examined.

Entrance to higher education has been widened by expanding facilities, and anybody who has passed the **Baccalauréat** (more commonly known as the '**Bac**') in the appropriate subjects can enrol for a university course. The prestigious Paris university, la Sorbonne, founded in 1209, has been divided into thirteen campuses – Paris I to Paris XIII – serving over 250,000 students. Each campus now has speciality subjects. In the provinces, many new institutions have been created to accommodate a greater number of students.

The Baccalauréat has been revised to offer the opportunity to specialise in technical fields, or alternatively to take the arts-based **lettres** course, or the general 'Bac'. In 1993 the pass rate was at 65 per cent. By 1997 this had risen to 78 per cent, still slightly short of the hoped-for pass rate of 80 per cent. The 'Bac' is equivalent to A-levels in Great Britain, and is the minimum that many employers require.

The Grandes Ecoles

For the real 'high-flyers', the French equivalent of 'Oxbridge' are the **Grandes Ecoles**, which are nonetheless outside of the university network. Some specialise in literature, some in science, and some in administration. Diplomas from these Ecoles are considered more prestigious than university degrees, and graduates normally are assured of high-level careers in business, public service or politics.

The most well-known Grandes Ecoles are the **Ecole Nationale d'Administration (ENA)** whose graduates are known as '**Enarchs**' and include former Prime Ministers Alain Juppé and Michel Rocard, President Chirac, and ex-President Giscard d'Estaing; the **Ecole Normale Supérieure**, whose alumni include François Mitterand; and the **Ecole Polytechnique**, also known as 'X', from which ex-President Giscard d'Estaing also graduated.

Opportunities for continuing education do exist in France depending on your geographical location. In Paris, the **mairies** (town halls) run language courses, and the Open University also now operates in France in the same way as in Great Britain. Professional training (**formation professionelle**) and qualifications are normally provided for in a company's budget (see Chapter 5).

APPRECIATING THE CULTURAL LIFE

The French heritage

In France culture and the pursuit of educated pleasure is highly regarded. France has always been known for its remarkable cultural heritage – from the Gothic masterpieces of Amiens, Bourges or Chartres cathedrals, to the Renaissance châteaux of the Loire Valley, or the splendours of the Sun King at Versailles, and on through the centuries ever since. It is a heritage that is to be found not simply carved in stone or gilded cherubs, but in music, literature and science.

The French are intensely and justly proud of their heritage, and you would do well to learn something of their cultural past in order not only to appreciate more deeply the new culture in which you find yourself, but also to share this great French passion. By understanding and sharing this cultural heritage with them, you will find that you are more quickly accepted into French society.

French pride in their culture can and does lead to tensions when they feel threatened. The opening in 1992 of a symbol of American culture on the doorstep of Paris, the EuroDisney park, was greeted with howls of protest by the intellectual community as a 'cultural Chernobyl'. There was a definite culture-clash, not just visually but mentally as the French found themselves exposed to American work-practices and commercialism of the kind they reject most deeply.

Five years on, tempers on both sides have cooled and the Disney experience is becoming more positive than negative. The opening of EuroDisney also coincided with a periodic French concern about the encroachments of Anglo-Saxon words into their language (safeguarded by the **Academie Française** who define words which are 'truly' French), and which led to a new law known as the **loi Toubon** after the minister who introduced it.

This continued concern demonstrates that the French cultural heritage is not simply a question of past glories. The modern arts are as greatly appreciated as their predecessors. The Centre Pompidou in Paris may repel you with its modernist tubular architecture, but it cannot be ignored. French cultural life is heavily supported from both central and private funds. Generous subsidies are given to the French film industry, and even cartoon artists have their own festival each year. Amongst the most famous occasions for demonstrating the French flair for creativity are the regular fashion shows in Paris which draw world-wide attention.

Nor is the cultural life of France restricted to the domineering influence of Paris. Many fine art museums (**Musées des Beaux-Arts**) in the provinces boast fine collections of paintings, and there are important opera houses in Bordeaux and Montpelier (where there are in fact two opera houses). Regional festivals are very common, most notably the festival of theatre at Avignon in the summer. Contemporary popular culture once again is not left unnoticed with the internationally known **Printemps de Bourges** (Spring Festival at Bourges). Many towns and villages now organise local arts festivals some of which draw international attention and support, such as the theatre festival at Avignon or the jazz festival at Souillac.

The Mitterand years
More than any other recent French leader, François Mitterand, who was President from 1981–1995, took on the mantle of a great cultural leader. Renowned for his intellect, bookishness and command of the French language, he chose the traditional method of great building schemes (**les grands travaux**) to attest to the glory of the country over which he reigned.

Mitterand left an indelible mark on Paris, with the Grand Arche at La Défense, the Pyramids at the Louvre which was totally reorganised and renovated during his presidency, the restored Tuileries gardens, the new opera house at the Bastille, and finally the new Bibliothèque Nationale which has ultimately been named in his honour. Nor was science neglected in favour of the visual and performing arts, with the completion of the adjoining Cités de Science et de la Musique at La Villette on the eastern edge of Paris.

Public holidays and fêtes

No introduction to France would be complete without mentioning the public holidays and **fêtes** (see Figure 2). It is important to know when these holidays occur, since many public services will shut down or run reduced services, whilst private commerce comes to a standstill. Transport is often heavily booked in advance at holiday periods.

Date	Occasion
1 January	New Year's Day – **Jour de l'An**
March/April	Easter Day and Easter Monday – **Pâques** N.B. Good Friday is not a holiday in France
1 May	Labour Day – **Fête du Travail**
8 May	Liberation Day – **Fête de la Libération**
May	Ascension Day – **l'Ascension** N.B. Date depends on the date of Easter
May/June	Pentecost/Whit Monday – **Pentecôte** N.B. Date depends on the date of Easter
14 July	National/Bastille Day – **Fête Nationale**
15 August	Feast of the Assumption – **l'Assomption**
1 November	All Saints Day – **Toussaint**
11 November	Remembrance Day – **Fête de la Victoire 1918**
25 December	Christmas Day – **Noël** N.B. 26 December is not a holiday in France

Fig. 2. Public holidays in France.

Although the provision of public holidays is generous, they are rigidly linked to the precise date. If a holiday falls on a Saturday or Sunday, then it is observed on that day, and no working day is given in lieu. However, if a holiday falls on either a Thursday or a Tuesday, then many people will take the link day to make a long weekend. This is known as **faire le pont** – literally to make a bridge.

The **Fête Nationale** (Bastille Day) on 14 July is always accompanied by huge public street parties in Paris and throughout France. Popular balls are organised at local fire-stations (**Bals des Sapeurs Pompiers**) on the night of 13 July. There are usually other free open-air parties not only in Paris but also in major cities. On 14 July, France parades her military glory along the Champs-Elysées under the President's scrutiny, before the traditional garden party at the Elysée Palace, and a magnificent son et lumière display near to the Eiffel Tower.

On 21 June each year (once again strictly observed on that date) is the newer **Fête de la Musique**. Although not a public holiday, it is an extremely popular occasion when free concerts are given in almost every church and café and seemingly on every street corner. The fête was created to encourage music-making (**faites de la musique** – a French play on words), and has been a tremendous success with vast open-air concerts in the major cities.

At the beginning of September each year are the traditional **Journées de la Patrimoine** (National Heritage weekend), commonly known as **les Portes-Ouvertes** (the 'Open Doors') Another recently invented festival, this is the annual occasion when the public can view the great state residences and buildings normally closed to the public, including the Elysée Palace in Paris, the Assemblée Nationale, and many Embassies usually on restricted access. Local **mairies** (town halls) will be able to tell you where to find lists of buildings which are open to the public. The concept of this festival has recently been imported to the United Kingdom.

2
Making Preparations

PREPARING THE PAPERWORK

Passports

Under the new internal arrangements (the Schengen Agreement) within the European Union (EU), citizens of the Union can enter France with just a National Identity Card. However, **British citizens need a valid British passport in order to enter France** (or indeed any other country covered by the Schengen Agreement), as the United Kingdom does not adhere to the Agreement.

Commonwealth citizens with residency rights in the UK are not recognised as British citizens under EU regulations. You will therefore be subject to entry requirements related to your country of origin. Channel Islanders and Manx citizens are not included either in the EU provisions, unless they or a parent or grandparent were born in the UK, or they have been resident in the UK for five years.

From October 1998, all children not already included on their parents' passports must have their own valid passport. This applies to new-born babies and infants, as well as older children.

Visas and residence permits

EU citizens do not require visas in order to enter France. Regulations for visas for non-EU citizens vary, and you will need to check current regulations with the French Embassy or Consulate nearest to you. For non-EU citizens, a number of different visas are available:

- **Visa de transit** – Allows three days travel across France by train.
- **Visa de circulation** – Often given to business people. This allows several stays of up to 90 days, with a maximum of 180 days in any one year. This visa is normally valid for three years.
- **Visa de court-séjour** – A short-stay visa valid for up to 90 days, permitting re-entry to France during that period.
- **Visa de long-séjour** – A long-stay visa for those studying, working or living in France for more than 90 days. You must already have this visa if you decide to stay for a longer period than originally

intended. Otherwise, you will be obliged to return to your home country in order to apply for this visa.

All foreigners intending to reside in France for more than three months must obtain a residence permit (**carte de séjour**). This includes EU and non-EU citizens. Temporary residence permits for non-EU nationals are normally valid for up to one year. For EU citizens, the temporary permit is normally valid for the length of your employment contract. See Chapter 3 for further details on how to apply for residence permits.

Driving papers

You are obliged to carry your papers with you whenever you are driving a vehicle in France. Failure to produce them can lead to a fine. You can bring a car into France for up to six months in any one year without having to complete customs formalities. See Chapter 9 for further details on licences, car importation and car registration.

Professional papers

Take with you all relevant professional certificates, diplomas, etc. which may be required if you are setting up your own business. You will also need to enquire at your nearest French Consulate about the **carte de commerçant** required in some cases by those seeking to create their own business.

Personal papers

You should bring with you copies of income tax documents for the last four years, and of any documents relating to investments and stocks and bonds. Receipts for your moving expenses, if they are not reimbursed by your employer, will be needed for tax purposes.

Pet papers

To import domestic pets, make sure that you have the animal's vaccination certificates and medical register up-to-date and ready for inspection. This should include a rabies vaccination certificate not more than six months old. Importing domestic cats and dogs into France is not difficult. However, if you have a pet snake or something else in that line, you will need to enquire about import regulations at the French Consulate.

The British Government has recently issued a consultation document on quarantine regulations for animals entering or re-entering the UK. There are six possible courses of action being considered, from no change at all, to free movement of animals with valid rabies vaccination certificates. It is unlikely that any new regulations would be implemented before the end of 1998.

DOCUMENT CHECKLIST

Check that you have all the following papers ready as you prepare for your departure:

1. Valid passport.

2. Valid visa for non-EU citizens.

3. Full certified copies of your birth certificate, that of your spouse, and those of your children.

4. Full certified copy of your marriage certificate.

5. Valid driving licence.

6. Car registration and insurance papers.

7. Carte de commerçant if this is required and professional certificates.

8. Au pairs should bring with them their Déclaration d'Engagement from their employer. Non-EU citizens may also be asked for a medical certificate.

9. Students should bring with them evidence of admission to a study course.

10. Bank statements, tax declarations and other financial documents. Proof of your financial resources may be demanded before you are granted a residence permit, depending on your nationality and occupation.

11. Vaccination certificates for your pets.

PREPARING TO MOVE HOME

Moving home is considered to be one of the most stressful experiences (after death and divorce) known to humanity! Moving your home abroad requires you to think carefully and methodically about what you do and do not need to take. A great deal will depend upon your own personal situation, but carefully planning will avoid unnecessary expense and complications.

Visiting your new home town

If you can, try visiting your new home town or city – and even better your new home! – before you make a move to France. Try and find out what sort of accommodation you will be able to afford on the salary and means at your disposal. In general, you will probably have less space in French accommodation than in an English house.

You will need to decide if you wish to rent furnished or unfurnished accommodation. If you are buying a new home in France but will keep your English home, consider if you can afford to furnish a new home completely. You must weigh this decision against the cost of removing certain items to, and later from, France.

Deciding what to take with you

- French kitchens are normally smaller than English kitchens, and you would probably be safer buying large kitchen machines and appliances (e.g. washing machines) within France.

- English electrical appliances do work in France. However, you must remember either to change the three-pin plug for a two-pin plug, or to buy adapters. English televisions and video recorders will not work in France, and these will need to be purchased or rented locally.

- Self-assembly furniture stores do readily exist in France, and buying furniture does not need to cost a fortune. You will need to decide if it is cheaper to buy furniture in France or to ship your own furniture to France. Furniture storage is generally very costly in France and the UK.

- French beds come in three standard sizes – single, small double and large double. Whilst your sheets and bedding will almost certainly fit these sizes, you should bear in mind that the standard French pillow is square not rectangular.

- Find out about the climate of the town or region to which you are moving, as regional variations in climate are very noticeable. You will need a fair share of winter and summer clothing if you are moving to France for a prolonged period. Clothes can be bought reasonably cheaply in France in high-street stores such as Monoprix or Prisunic if both your budget and your storage facilities are limited. Figure 3 gives conversion sizes for English and French clothes measurements.

	Men's suits	Men's shirts	Men's shoes
UK	36 38 40 42 44 46 48	14 14.5 15 15.5 16 16.5 17	7 7.5 8.5 9.5 10.5 11
France	46 48 50 52 54 56 58	36 37 38 39/40 41 42 43	41 42 43 44 45 46

	Dress sizes	Women's shoes	
UK	8 10 12 14 16 18	4.5 5 5.5 6 6.5 7	
France	36 38 40 42 44 46	38 38 39 39 40 41	

Fig. 3. Clothes size conversions.

IMPORT RULES AND REGULATIONS

Detailed rules about the importation of household goods should be discussed with the customs sections of the French consulate. If you use a professional moving firm, they should also be able to inform you about necessary customs formalities.

- For EU citizens, goods on which you have already paid VAT in another EU member country are exempt from VAT payments when imported into France. This should be specified on the 'CMR' form provided by a professional removal firm. If you have receipts which show that VAT has already been paid, it is wise to have these available for inspection if required. You should also prepare an itemised inventory of your effects, both for customs inspection, and in case of an insurance claim.

- Non-EU citizens are also exempt from VAT payments on their belongings, *providing that* they have been in their possession more than six months, *and* that VAT has been paid in another EU country. You will be required by the French customs officials to produce receipts to this effect. Items purchased less than six months before your arrival, and/or outside the EU area, will be subject to VAT payment. You have one year from the date of your arrival in France to import your possessions before they become subject to VAT payment.

- Arrangements for the importation of vehicles are given in Chapter 9.

- There are restrictions on which plants can be imported into France (particular varieties of 'herbs' and 'pot plants' are not appreciated ...), although a limited number of plants can be included amongst your personal effects. If in doubt, contact the Service de la Protection des Végétaux, 175 rue de Chevaleret, 75646 Paris Cedex 13. Tel: 01 45 84 13 13.

• Works of art and collectors' items may require special import licences, and firearms and ammunition also. Medicines and medical products, except for prescribed drugs, may also be subject to special regulations. For all these items, you must contact the French Consulate for further information. You can also contact the French customs office at the Centre Renseigne-ment des Douanes, 238 quai de Bercy, 75572 Paris Cedex 12. Tel: 01 40 01 02 06.

PREPARING FINANCIALLY

It can cost a lot of money to set up your new home in France. If you rent an apartment or house, you will have to pay two months' rent in advance as a deposit (and up to three months for commercial premises), and also the rent for the first month – i.e. three months' rent in advance.

If you use an agency to find your new home, there will also be their fee to pay, normally equivalent to one month's rent. You will then have the cost of electricity and gas connections, and the rental of a telephone line to pay as well.

It can be difficult to secure a rental contract from French landlords especially if you are a foreigner. Even young French couples are asked for written guarantees, from either their parents or their employers, as a precaution against unpaid rents and bills. Make sure that you bring a significant sum of money with you to cover both these initial expenses, and day-to-day living expenses. Driving licences and residence permits also have to be paid for.

PREPARING CULTURALLY

Many people come to France specifically to improve their French, or quite simply to learn the language for the first time. You will find that a grasp of the most basic phrases and words will help you enormously when you arrive. Do not count on 'everybody speaking English' to you; many can, but not everybody will. You will certainly need to understand what is being said to you when you apply for your residence permit, for example.

You will integrate more rapidly and increase your own personal standing with French people if they see that you are trying your best to communicate with them in their own language.

- Try hard to find time to study basic grammar, phrases and vocabulary before you come to France. If you have the opportunity, an evening or conversation class would be a very good idea.

- Bring a good dictionary with you (not necessarily the most expensive), and also a good phrase book.

You should also try to find out something about the country to which you are moving. There are plenty of excellent introductions to French history and culture available in bookshops in the UK and indeed throughout the world. The varied and generally very good French press is also widely available. Reading articles on current life in France will not only help you understand your new environment, but will also improve your language skills.

CHECKLIST

1. Have you gathered together all the necessary papers? See the Document Checklist (page 42) to be sure.

2. What are the most essential items you will need when you arrive in your new home?

3. Have you made sufficient financial provision for the first few months in France?

3
Arriving and Settling In

ARRIVING IN FRANCE

Very many people will arrive at their final destination in France via Paris. If you are intending to take a ferry or another route into France, make sure of your intended route and travel plans before leaving. Help can be obtained from the French Tourist Office at 179 Piccadilly in London, where there is also a French national railway office which sells tickets in advance and which can also help with timetables and connections.

Arriving by air
Paris is served by two international airports. Roissy-Charles-de-Gaulle is fourteen miles to the north of the capital and Orly is nine miles to the south. Most international airlines have direct services to Paris. Buses leave about every fifteen minutes from the airport for the centre of Paris.

- **From Roissy** you can either take the Air France bus to Porte Maillot and the Arc de Triomphe (Place de l'Etoile), or the 'Roissy Bus' to rue Scribe next to the Place de l'Opéra. Both services take about forty-five minutes depending on traffic, and cost about 50 FF.

- **From Orly** you can take the Air France bus to Les Invalides Terminal.

Buses back to the airports leave from these same places at about the same frequency every day. There are also public buses and train services between the airports and Paris. Both airports are served by RER Ligne B (see below), and journey time is about 40 minutes from central Paris.

Taxis are available twenty-four hours a day at the airports. If the taxi driver asks for a return fare, refuse – it is illegal. Car rental facilities are also available at the airports. If you drive take the motorway (**autoroute**) A1 from Roissy or A6 from Orly. A shuttle bus service between the airports takes about one hour.

Arriving by Eurostar

You will arrive at Paris-Gare du Nord in central Paris, which serves not only northern France and Eurostar services, but also other northern European destinations. You should pay particular attention to your belongings at this station, especially at night when it can be dangerous.

The station is served by numerous public buses, the RER and métro (see below), and the local railway system for the Paris suburbs. Taxis are available only at the taxi rank. Follow the signs down to the rank. There are also Eurostar services direct to Brussels, and to the EuroDisney park east of Paris.

Arriving from the Channel ports

If you take the ferry to Boulogne, Calais or Dunkerque, the connecting train to Paris will arrive at Paris-Gare du Nord (see above). If you take the ferry to Caen, Cherbourg, Dieppe or Le Havre, the connecting train to Paris will arrive at Paris-St Lazare. This station is similar to Gare du Nord in almost all respects, but more central and a little safer at night.

Eurotunnel Terminal for Le Shuttle

Le Shuttle leaves from Folkestone and arrives at Calais-Fréthun. Once you have disembarked from the train, and completed the usual immigration and customs formalities, you will be free to leave the station and to take the road to your destination.

Arriving by coach

The coach from Victoria Station in London remains probably the cheapest option for crossing the Channel. However, it is also now the longest. Coaches arrive at Bagnolet on the eastern edge of Paris. Métro line 3 runs nearby and the nearest station is Gallieni. This line will take you rapidly to the heart of central Paris.

Always take care of your personal possessions and do not entrust them to a stranger even for a moment. Always take care over your personal safety at travel centres. Beware of pickpockets and keep travel documents and cash safely concealed.

USING WELCOME CENTRES

The main Paris Tourist Office (**office de tourisme**) is at 127 avenue des Champs-Elysées, 75008 Paris. The nearest métro station is Charles-de-Gaulle-Etoile, next to the Arc de Triomphe and near to the bus stops to Roissy airport. Information offices and welcome centres (**services d'acceuil**) can also be found at the airports, and in all major railway stations: Gare de Lyon, Gare d'Austerlitz, Gare de l'Est, Gare du Nord and Gare St Lazare. All of these centres will be able to provide practical information and help including hotel reservation services.

Most French towns have a tourist office (**office de tourisme** or **syndicat d'initiative**) which can help with hotel and travel arrangements, as well as informing you about local excursions and events.

GETTING AROUND PARIS

Paris is divided into twenty **arrondissements** or districts. You need to know the numbers of the arrondissements to find out where to go, and the French refer to them often in conversation. Public transport is frequent, extensive and not expensive. It is well worth taking advantage of the variety of means of transport available.

Using the métro
The Parisian underground system, the métro, is one of the best in the world. Stations are close together, and trains run twenty hours a day from 05h30 until 01h30. Generally the métro is clearly marked, well-lit, quiet and clean. The basic structure of the métro is a series of concentric circles with spokes at intervals, enabling you to change from one line to another. One ticket is good for the length of any one trip. It is cheaper to buy a book of ten tickets (**carnet**) than to buy tickets individually.

RER or Rapid Regional Transit
The RER (**Réseau Express Régional**) is a more recent and very modern system with underground trains running deeper than the métro. It is an express system with fewer stops, but which reaches much further out into the Paris suburbs. Fares vary according to distance, and the RER runs from 05h30 until midnight. A number of central métro stations have intersections with the RER.

Using the local railway service
The French state railway company (SNCF – **Société Nationale des Chemins de Fer**) runs local services with frequent stops in the suburbs (**banlieues**) or Paris. These operate at roughly the same times as the RER and métro.

Travelling by bus
There is an excellent bus network in Paris. The right lane of the streets is reserved for buses, so buses move fairly well. Passengers line up at the bus stop (**arrêt**) as in the UK. Inside the bus there is a chart of the route and the stops, with information on how many tickets are needed for each distance travelled. Timetables are posted at bus stops. Certain lines run until 0h30 in the morning, but mostly the last bus is at 21h00.

Bus and métro tickets are identical. However, you cannot purchase a **carnet** of tickets from the bus driver.

There are a number of night-buses (**noctambus**) which serve Paris, leaving from the Place du Chatelet every hour on the half-hour (e.g. 01h30, 02h30), until the métro opens once again at 05h30. You can use your **Carte Orange** pass on these buses (see below), but you cannot use ordinary bus tickets. Purchase tickets from the driver.

Keep hold of your ticket in the bus, RER and métro. If there is a ticket check (*contrôle*) and you do not have your ticket, you could face an on-the-spot fine of more than 200 FF.

Maps of the bus, RER and métro systems are available free in métro stations at the ticket office, and at tourist offices.

Carte Orange and other passes
The Carte Orange is the Paris Travelcard covering bus, métro and RER. There are six zones, and the price varies according to the number of zones you wish to include. Zones 1 and 2 cover the whole of central Paris, up to the end of almost all métro lines. Check at your local station to see which zone you live in.

When you buy your Carte for the first time, take one passport-size photo with you, and ask for a *coupon orange*. Stick the photo to this, fill in your name and address, and write the number of the coupon on the white ticket printed with the month and the date. Otherwise, the Carte Orange is invalid and you could face a heavy fine.

You will be supplied with a small holder for the coupon and the carte, and you can ask for a free métro map at the same time to insert into the back of the holder. Always remember to take back your ticket once you have passed through the métro or RER barriers. Never put your ticket into the punching machine on buses, but do show the pass to the driver. You can also buy a similar weekly pass (**carte hebdomodaire**).

There are a number of other passes available for tourists each year which give unlimited travel for a period of days. Ask about these at any métro station, or at your hotel or welcome centre.

Getting around by bike

One unexpected result of the strikes in 1995 was that the French became very keen on cycling around their capital city. Bike lanes have been laid out across the city, and are constantly being extended. These run from the forests on the east and west of the city, and along the busiest streets right across the commercial centre.

Using taxis

In Paris, like everywhere else in the world, taxis are harder to find in rush hour or bad weather. You can normally find a taxi by simply hailing one down on a busy main street, or by going to a **Station de Taxi** (taxi rank). You will often find taxis waiting for fares outside nightclubs, well-known hotels or theatres.

In Paris, when the sign on top of the cab is lit up, the taxi is for hire. When it is not, the taxi is occupied. If you have ordered the taxi, the meter will be running when the taxi arrives, as you pay for the service from the moment the driver has accepted the call to collect you. Make sure if you catch a taxi in the street that the previous fare has been cleared from the meter. Day and night rates should be displayed, and many taxi drivers will have standard rates for a trip to one of the airports near Paris. Tipping is generally 10–15 per cent.

Finally bear in mind that all taxis will take three passengers, but very few will accept four passengers. Extra charges are made for large amounts of luggage.

Car rental

Car rental can be arranged prior to your departure, either through local agents of the large companies, or through airlines and other transport companies. Most of the major companies have agencies in

France. Rental prices vary from company to company, and depend on the size and make of the car. VAT at 20.6 per cent (called TVA in France) is added to the hire price. Rates do not include fuel, collision or personal accident insurance. Ask about the cover provided when you hire a car. Generally the hirer is responsible for collision damage to a rented vehicle.

MONEY MATTERS

French money

The French franc is divided into 100 centimes. It is abbreviated to FF to distinguish it from the Swiss franc (SF) and the Belgian franc (BF). Obtain a selection of French money from a bank or foreign currency exchange before leaving for France. It is a good idea to familiarise yourself with the different coins and notes before you arrive in France. Notes and coins exist in the following denominations:

- **Notes** (or bills): 20, 50, 100, 200 and 500 francs. Beware of forgeries, and check for water-marks. Many shops now have detectors which recognise forged notes.

- **Coins**: 5, 10, 20, 50 centimes; 1, 2, 5, 10 and 20 francs.

Currency exchange offices are located in airports, railway stations and most banks. If you have the time and the choice, compare exchange rates to find the most favourable rate, and also check to see how much commission you will be charged. In central Paris, you will find many currency exchanges centred around the rue Scribe and the Place de l'Opera near the bus stops for Roissy airport.

French banks

There are four principal French banks: Banque Nationale de Paris (BNP), Crédit Agricole, Crédit Lyonnais and Société Générale. Of the major Anglo-Saxon banks, Barclays is the best represented in France with about 100 branches in Paris and across France.

To gain access to banks in France, press the bell outside the street door. When the green light flashes, enter and wait until the door closes. Then press the second bell, and open the door when the second green light flashes. Follow the system in reverse to get out again. Despite the security, the atmosphere inside is normally more relaxed!

Opening times

French banks are generally open from 09h00 to 16h30 Monday to

Friday. Many French banks in cities and large towns are now also open on Saturdays. Lunch hours generally run from 12h30 until 14h00. They are closed on all public holidays, and may close for **le pont** (see Chapter 1 on public holidays). In smaller country towns, banks may close on Mondays if they are open on Saturdays.

Opening a French bank account

You will become accustomed to red tape and paperwork in France. However, opening a bank account is one of the easiest steps to take. There are two options:

- **A non-resident account (compte non-résident).** Previously there were many restrictions on these accounts. However, these restrictions generally do not apply any longer. But whilst you can negotiate loans to buy a car or a house, you may not have an overdraft facility (**découverts**). This facility would be appropriate if you buy a second home in France.

- **An ordinary current account.** If you are resident in France, or are working principally in France, then you will normally be able to open a current account entitling you to a cheque book and a **carte bleue**, the standard French credit card.

To open your account, take the following original items, plus copies of each:

- passport, or residence permit (for resident accounts)
- proof of address (**justicatif de domicile**) – this can either be a copy of your rental agreement, or a telephone or electricity bill with your name and address on it.

You will sign customary account-opening forms and give a specimen signature to permit the payment of cheques written by you.

Understanding how the system operates

- Some banks may make you wait to receive your **carte bleue**. However, they will give you a cash card which will allow you to use the bank's automatic cash machines. You can use your card not only to withdraw cash, but also to give you a statement of the balance of your account (**solde**), and also a statement of the most recent transactions on your account (**relevé**). Some banks also offer other services such as ordering cheque books, paying in cheques, etc.

● Cheques normally take about three days to clear once they have been paid into an account. This can take longer if they are drawn on an account (**compensable**) in a more distant town or city, or from another bank. Nonetheless, the date that will appear on your monthly statement (**relevé de compte**) is the date on which the cheque was deposited into your account.

● Cheques are used almost as frequently as cash in France for payment. To fill out a French cheque, write the amount in figures in the top right-hand corner, and then the words on the first (and second if necessary) line(s) of the cheque. Then fill out the name or company to whom you wish to pay the cheque. Remember to sign the cheque in the space provided on the bottom right-hand corner, and to fill in the date and town where you wrote the cheque.

  Many shops now have machines which automatically fill out the amount of the cheque, date, place and to whom it is payable. You can cash a cheque at any branch of your own bank. Simply make it payable to yourself. **A piece of official identification is normally required to endorse cheques, and is always required when cashing a cheque in the bank**. There are no cheque cards in France.

● Cheques can only be stopped in France in the case of loss or theft of your cheque book. They cannot be stopped because of unsatisfactory goods or services.

● A cash deposit into your account (**versement d'especes**) will normally be registered much more rapidly than a cheque deposit. Banks normally have a separate counter (**guichet**) for cash deposits and withdrawals.

● Direct debits (**prélèvements**) can be used to pay for many services in France, including taxes, electricity bills, telephone bills and rent.

● **It is illegal to be overdrawn in France without a prior agreement with the bank, or to exceed your overdraft limit. There can be serious consequences if you break this rule.** You may be placed on the Debtors List at the Banque de France, and be refused credit in the future.

- There is no reason at all why you should close your bank account in your home country. It is probably a good idea to keep a reserve sum of money in your national currency in order to avoid conversion rates when you return home.

- You should also consider opening a deposit account in order to save for tax bills (which for the first year are a large lump sum) or to provide yourself with some form of security in time of trouble.

Using credit cards

The principal French credit card is the **carte bleue visa**, issued by all major French banks. This will give you the right to draw money from all cash machines in France, and is the most widely recognised and used of all cards. As with cheques, the carte bleue widely replaces cash. Payment is normally accepted from 100 FF. You will have your own PIN number, which not only gives access to machines, but is also essential for paying for goods in shops and restaurants.

The carte bleue is debited immediately, and is not a credit card in 'the true sense'. Standard credit cards are generally accepted, with Visa being the most widely accepted. If the sign of your own credit card is not displayed at the entrance to a restaurant, you may wish to check it is accepted *before* spending any money! Many stores and commercial groups have account credit cards.

Some British credit cards without micro-chips are refused in France, although they *are* valid. If your card is refused, you should politely insist.

> **IF YOU LOSE YOUR CARD OR IT IS STOLEN:**
> **Telephone 01 45 67 84 84. This number can now be found on most cash machines if the card is stolen whilst you are out. You must cancel the card immediately, and report the loss or theft to the police, and to your bank. All this should be done as quickly as possible to avoid fraudulent use of your card. French banks will arrange a replacement carte bleue fairly rapidly.**

Tipping

There are no definite tipping rules, but generally the following people are tipped: porters, taxi drivers, doormen, room service, waiters, cloakroom attendants, hairdressers and lavatory attendants. Taxi drivers are usually given 10–15 per cent and hairdressers 10 per cent. In restaurants the service is usually included, in which case the bill will read 'TTC' (**toutes taxes comprises**).

If you have received good service, it is customary to leave a tip nonetheless for the waiter. Never leave centimes as a tip. This is considered very insulting, and it would be better to leave no tip at all than to leave centimes.

You should tip the **concierge** of your apartment building at Christmas, depending on the level of service you have received from them. This is an 'annual tip' and should be in the region of 150 FF depending on your financial capacity. Should you live in a small garret at the top of the building, a smaller gift will be equally appreciated. Around Christmas, others will call on you for their 'Christmas Box' – postmen, refuse collectors and the local firemen. You are not obliged to give money to these people, and such collections are strictly speaking illegal. However, it is up to you to decide on the level of your own personal generosity.

INTRODUCING THE SINGLE CURRENCY (THE EURO)

On 1 January 1999, there will be a Europe-wide financial and cultural revolution. France is one of the principal countries leading the introduction of the single European currency, which will be known as the **Euro**. The Ministry of Economy, Finance and Industry has published a free leaflet available in all banks and post offices explaining how and when the new currency will be introduced.

From 1 January 1999 until 1 January 2002, both French francs and the Euro will be common currency in France. Prices, salaries, rents and taxes will all be published in both currencies, as banks and businesses make the conversions necessary for the total abolition of the French franc on 1 January 2002. The French stock market will operate only in Euros from 1 January 1999.

The exact value of the Euro will be announced on 1 January 1999. At the moment, one Euro is approximately equal to 6.50 FF. On 1 January 2002 at the latest, the conversion to the Euro will be complete, and all financial transactions will take place in Euros. All French currency will be replaced by new coins and notes.

- **Notes** (or bills): 5, 10, 20, 50, 100, 200 and 500 Euros. Any remaining French franc notes can be exchanged for Euros at the Banque de France until 1 January 2012.

- **Coins**: 1 and 2 Euros, and 1, 2, 5, 10, 20, 50 cents (equivalent to centimes, representing one hundredth of Euros). French cents will still carry the mark RF to distinguish them as coins issued in France.

On 1 January 2002, all bank accounts will be automatically converted into Euros. All existing financial contracts and arrangements will automatically remain valid, but will be calculated in the new currency. Cartes bleues will permit you to withdraw Euros from cash machines.

The Euro will be valid in all countries which participate in the European Monetary Union scheme. At first this will be a core group of eleven countries, principally composed of France, Germany and the Benelux countries. The scheme allows for other countries to join the system when they meet certain economic criteria. The United Kingdom will not be a founder member of the Euro currency.

Information about the Euro can be obtained in France on a free help-line telephone number: 0800 01 2002, or on the Internet at httpp://www.finances.gouv.fr/euro.

REGISTERING AT YOUR EMBASSY

British citizens are not required to register at the embassy or the nearest consulate-general. However, if you use the consular services for other reasons (e.g. information purposes), it may be as well to register.

When you arrive in France, you will need to obtain a **Fiche d'état civile**, which is an official document translated by an officially recognised translator which will combine translations of your birth certificate, your marriage certificate, the birth certificate of your spouse, and the birth certificates of your children.

This service is offered in Paris by your country's consulate, at a fee. Ring and check the price in advance. In the suburbs and provinces it can also be performed at the local town hall (**mairie**), where a fee will also be charged. You must use one of these two services, and not a private translator. You will need to bring with you:

- Your passport, and that of your spouse and children if they are to be included on the same Fiche.

- A salmon-coloured 'certified' copy of your birth certificate, obtained from the registry office in the UK where your birth was registered. You will also need similar copies of your spouse's and children's birth certificates if they are to be included on the same Fiche.

- A green-coloured 'certified' copy of your marriage certificate if applicable, obtained from either the church or the registry office in the UK where your marriage was registered.

N.B. Photocopies are not acceptable. It must be an 'original' certified copy. You need your Fiche d'état civile in order to apply for your social security card and residence permit. Children born in France should be registered immediately in order to preserve the child's claim to native citizenship. New passports can be obtained via your consulate. Principal consulates and embassies in France are listed in the Regional Directory at the end of this book.

OBTAINING YOUR RESIDENCE PERMIT

If you intend to stay in France for more than three months, you must apply for a residence permit (**carte de séjour**). Failure to apply for your permit within three months of arrival is a serious offence.

- **Citizens of a member country of the European Union (EU)** have a right to a residence permit if they have a job in France, or can prove they have the financial resources to support themselves. The permit will normally initially be valid for five years, unless the holder has a temporary job with a contract for a year or less. EU citizen rights are not granted to Australians with British residency rights, and there are certain restrictions on inhabitants of the Channel Islands and the Isle of Man. You must have a full British passport in order to qualify. You can either apply by post or in person for a carte de séjour.

- **Citizens of non-EU countries** need a long-term visa (**visa de long séjour**) before arrival in France (see Chapter 2). Residence permits will not be issued without the appropriate visas. Americans and Canadians do not need entry visas for France, but Australians do need entry visas.

  - In Paris you will need to ask your consulate which police centre (**centre d'acceuil des étrangers**) you need to apply to. The centre will be different according to where you live.

– Outside Paris, you should initially apply to the local town hall (**mairie**) who may refer you to a **Préfecture** (police headquarters) for that département.

The bureaucracy you encounter to obtain your carte can be agony. It is advisable to take several copies of all your documents with you, and a good book to read, and allow plenty of time. You will receive a temporary carte (**récipissé de demande de carte de séjour**) initially, proving you have applied and valid for three months. This will eventually be replaced by your permanent carte.

CHECKLIST: DOCUMENTS NEEDED TO OBTAIN YOUR CARTE DE SÉJOUR

The following is a list of documents which are usually required no matter what your nationality or status. **Regulations often change, so check the precise requirements with your local préfecture or mairie.**

1. Your full birth certificate (the salmon-pink 'certified' copy you used for your Fiche d'état civile).

2. Your passport.

3. Your Fiche d'état civile.

4. Four passport-sized black-and-white photographs.

5. Either the rental contract on your apartment, or a bill from France Télécom or Électricité de France (EDF) in your name showing your address.

6. Either a salary slip from your employer, or your **lettre d'embauche** (job offer) on headed paper from your employer.

LEARNING THE LANGUAGE

In order to get the most out of your time in France, you simply **must** study French and learn to speak it as well as you possibly can. If you do not, you will almost certainly find yourself considerably restricted and you will definitely feel left out. The French place a very high priority on their language, and their opinion of you as a foreigner will depend to a significant degree on whether you speak their language. Although they may criticise your less-than-perfect attempts to speak French, they will respect you far more for having tried than if you insist on speaking English.

There are now literally hundreds of language schools in and around Paris, and indeed throughout France. They provide tuition at all levels, from basic to advanced, and many offer courses in Business French. Try looking in the *Yellow Pages* (**pages jaunes**) or the local phonebook. Welcome offices, consulates, churches and clubs often have details or advertisements from schools and private tutors. You may prefer to use a private tutor at first if you are shy of speaking French in public.

You may also see offers of 'conversation exchange', whereby you trade-off an hour of English for an hour of French conversation. This could be a good way to meet people also, and you could try joining a conversation group.

Try and listen to as much French TV and radio as possible, so that you start to become used to the sound of the language, and the way in which it is used. Also, try reading one of the more accessible French newspapers such as *Libération* or *France-Soir*, in order to develop your vocabulary.

When you go shopping, read everything, paying particular attention to labels. Make an effort to go to some small local shops, and learn to pay for the items you buy. After a while you will be able to carry on a simple conversation with the shopkeepers, who are often happy to help and advise their loyal customers.

Finally, do not be afraid to make mistakes (**faux pas**). Use French whenever you can, and try to forget the natural dread of saying the wrong thing. A sense of humour is essential, and the ability to laugh at your own mistakes.

Mastering the French language is a question of confidence, no matter what level you are starting from. Just as when you learn to walk you must expect to stumble every now and then, so when you are learning to speak French you must not be too upset by unintentional errors. By and large, your efforts will be rewarded with respect, an understanding smile, and a little patient help.

COMMUNICATIONS

Public telephones
Coin-operated telephones are now only found in cafés, hotels, restaurants and some cinemas. Otherwise, all public telephones are generally operated by phone-card (**télécarte**), sold in post offices and

Fig. 4. Telephone area codes.

tobacconists (**tabacs**). Rates are cheaper after 21h30, on official holidays and Sundays. Long-distance rates vary according to distance. Local-call rates normally offer fairly generous amounts of time for the rate charged.

France is divided into five area codes, numbered from 01 (Paris) to 05 (for the south west). (See Figure 4.) Dial the area code + the eight-figure number to reach your correspondent. For international calls dial 00 + country code + city code + telephone number.

Mobile phones

With over 3.5 million subscribers by June 1997, France has finally caught the mobile phone habit. There are a wide variety of systems available covering the whole country, including well-known British makes. If you bring a British-based mobile phone to France, remember the following rules for use:

- To make a call, dial as if you are a local subscriber. Dial your correspondent's number in the same way as you would do on a normal telephone. Include international dialling codes where appropriate.

- **Calls made to other British-based mobile phones must be made using the international dialling codes, even if your correspondent is also in France.** For instance, if you are in Caen, and you want to call your friend in Paris who has a British-based mobile phone, dial 00 44, then your friend's normal mobile phone number but without the 0 at the beginning of the number.

Call-back systems

Call-back systems are readily available in France. Details of subscription rates and services can be found in 'international' magazines. Savings on international rates are often at least 30 per cent.

Understanding the postal system

As in the UK, post offices offer many more services than simply the post. Main post offices are normally open 08h00–19h00 Monday–Friday, and from 0800–noon on Saturdays. In Paris, the main post office in the rue du Louvre is open 24 hours. Stamps can also be purchased at tobacconist's shops.

Automatic franking machines inside post offices, including scales for weighing letters and small packages, dispense labels (**etiquettes**) for the appropriate value. Using these can help you to avoid the often considerable queues for assistance at the counter. Postage rates differ with destination and weight.

If you wish to send a registered letter (**lettre recommandé**), there are a number of options:

- with no proof of delivery and no declared value, but with a proof of despatch – **sans avis de réception**

- with proof of delivery (which will be sent back to you signed and dated), a proof of despatch, but no declared value – **avec accusé de réception**

- with declared value – **avec valeur declarée**.

Chronopost is the French equivalent of Datapost in the UK, and next-day delivery is normally guaranteed throughout France. France uses a 5-digit code system, with the code written before the name of the town or city. The first two digits indicate the département, and the last three indicate the city. For instance: the eighth arrondissement of Paris is 75008 (75 for Paris, 008 for the eighth arrondissement).

Using fax

All regular fax services are available throughout France, including both Group 3, and the faster but rarer Group 4. You can easily have a fax line installed in your home or office, but the machine must be 'approved' (**agréé**) by France Télécom. All the major fax distributors are present in France.

Most major towns and cities have shops where fax machines can be rented or purchased, from smaller phone-fax machines through to larger laser printer machines. If you buy or rent a machine, check on the cost and availability of after-sales service and of supplies.

Using the Internet

France is well-connected to all major Internet systems and services, and is participating fully in the multi-media revolution of the late 1990s. This is both through home-grown material, and a strong American presence in the French market. You should have no problem connecting your existing equipment to French outlets. Several 'cyber cafés' have recently opened in central Paris, allowing consumers to surf the net over lunch or a coffee.

Minitel

It is no great surprise that France has welcomed the Internet so quickly. In 1981, the French equivalent of Prestel was launched, known as Minitel. It is now the largest such system in the world, and has recently been updated in the face of competition from new services.

A terminal with a keyboard is connected to the phone, and allows the user to obtain all manner of information, from train times to share prices; to pay bills; or even to make dinner or concert ticket reservations. It also serves as an electronic telephone directory. Minitels are available for public consultation in main post offices. Most French people have one installed in their home.

Pay attention to how much you use the Minitel. The cost per minute of a call is very much higher than an ordinary telephone call. Remember that you are paying for a service of convenience.

THE MEDIA

Radio

Under French law, at least 40 per cent of air-time every day must be devoted to French music on commercial music radio stations. There are a wide variety of stations available throughout France. The leading 'classic' radio stations are *France-Inter* (current events, music and discussions), *France-Culture* (arts and literature), and *France-Musique* (classical music and jazz).

In Paris, if you buy a copy of *Pariscope* at any kiosk, you will instantly have a free frequency guide to all the major Parisian radio stations at the back of the magazine. For those who are pining for the cricket commentary or *The Archers*, it is relatively easy to receive the BBC World Service and Radio 4 throughout France.

Television

Foreign TV sets do not work in France, so you will need to buy or rent when you arrive. There are six TV channels available throughout France:

- *TF1* is privately owned. It generally has the 'big name' news presenters and TV journalists. Otherwise, the quality of programmes is variable, with many poor quality game shows and '**realité**' shows (e.g. tracing missing relatives, etc.).

- *France 2* is still state owned. This is the main heavyweight rival to TF1. There is a generally higher standard of varied programmes.

- *FR3* is also still state owned. They produce regional programmes and news reports. Programming is similar to France 2.

- *Canal +* is a private pay channel. For part of the day everybody is able to receive their programmes, and part of the day (normally the most interesting part) you must take out a private subscription for a receiver. Many good quality films and the popular satirical puppet show *Les Guignols* appear on Canal +.

- *La Cinque/Arte* – these two stations share a frequency, Arte taking over at 19h00. The latter is a Franco-German company. An intellectual channel, with good documentaries, no game shows, and films in original languages (**version originale** or **v.o.**) including English. They also show English comedy series in v.o.

- *M6* is considered a 'lightweight' channel in comparison with the others. Nonetheless there is a good selection of films and reports, and a much younger dynamic feel to the presentation.

On French TV there is a coding system with different symbols on the screen indicating the level of parental consent advisable for various films and programmes. The main programme for the evening normally begins about 20h45, after the news and weather broadcast.

Satellite television, offering a wide variety of channels from sport to history, and including the BBC and leading American channels, is now widely available throughout France. Check to find out if your building is cabled (**cablé**), and ask neighbours about how and where to subscribe.

Newspapers and magazines

France has a very wide variety of newspapers and magazines. Regional newspapers are often given greater prominence in France than is the case in the UK. The principal national French newspapers are:

- *Le Figaro* – right-wing, conservative

- *Le Monde* – independent, centre-left, regarded as 'the intellectual's newspaper' for both the right-wing and the left-wing

- *Libération* – young, centre-left and trendy

- *L'Humanité* – the mouthpiece of the Communist party

- *France-Soir* – sensational headlines, most akin to the English tabloids

- *Le Canard Enchainé* – the scourge of the political establishment, satirical but serious.

Les Echoes and *La Tribune* are the business newspapers (equivalent to *The Financial Times*); *L'Equipe* is the popular sports newspaper; *La Croix* is run by the French Catholic Church. Magazines such as *L'Evenement du jeudi*, *L'Express* and *Le Nouvel Observateur* offer good broad-ranging weekly news coverage.

The foreign press is widely available each and every day in France, but at a more elevated cost. One way to save money is to take out a subscription to your favourite newspaper, which often leads to considerable savings. Telephone the newspaper of your choice before leaving to ask about subscriptions if you will be in France for a considerable length of time.

ADJUSTING TO PATTERNS OF LIVING

Times and dates

In France, the 24-hour clock is used; for example 1.20pm is written as 13h20, 8.00am is 8h00, and 5.30pm is 17h30. The French working day usually begins at 9h00 and finishes at 18h00. The long French lunch hour is still widely observed from 12h30 until 14h00. Even if only a shorter period is actually taken for lunch, many offices will be closed to the public during this whole period.

Early mornings are generally busy with the rush to the office or school, but less so in the school holidays. It is a good idea to buy yourself a French diary which lists the school holidays and French bank holidays. School holiday dates vary from region to region, and bank holidays considerably affect work patterns (see Chapter 1).

Shopping

Once the workers have reached their offices and the children have reached their schools, shopping begins. In France it is quite common to buy fresh food provisions every day from the local market (**le marché**) or small neighbourhood shops. The main ones you will need to find are:

the baker	**(la boulangerie)**
the butcher	**(la boucherie)**
the cheese shop	**(la fromagerie)**
the grocer	**(l'épicerie)**
the delicatessen	**(la charcuterie)**

Shopping in French markets is a real joy, and the choice of produce and prices is generally excellent. It is also another good way of learning new vocabulary. Don't forget that France is a metric country, and that quantities are given in kilos (one pound = 0.45kg).

Supermarkets (**le supermarché**) are often open until 20h00, and do not close at lunchtime. The smaller shops and the market stalls will close between about 13h00 and 15h30, but they will then stay open until about 19h00. In Paris, markets are often open on Sunday mornings, but closed all day Monday.

You will need to buy fresh bread most mornings, especially the traditional **baguette** which does not stay fresh overnight. The boulangeries open early – around 07h30 – and do not close until about 19h00. But rush at the end of the day if you want to be sure of buying bread to eat with dinner. If you want to buy loaves of bread, which come in many varieties, you can ask to have them sliced (**coupé**), for which you will pay a few centimes extra. Kept in sealed plastic, these loaves will last several days.

Lunchtime in France will see mothers or au pairs collecting children from school for lunch at home before the afternoon session. For office workers, lunch is normally now restricted to one hour, often spent in a nearby café. In the evening, dinner is normally eaten at about 20h00 or slightly later. You should avoid telephoning people at this time of night unless it is absolutely necessary.

The pace of life outside Paris is much less hectic than in the capital. The long lunch hour is more normally observed in the country, including the business closing time.

The weekend

No matter where you are in France, everybody looks forward to the weekend after a busy week at work or school. This is the time grandparents expect to see their children, if they have not been whisked away to a second home in the country. Do-it-yourself (**bricolage**) is increasingly popular as a form of relaxation at the weekend, and sport in all its forms is very popular, as well as the traditional cultural pursuits and the Sunday afternoon stroll.

The concierge

Finally, there is one person with whom you should definitely make friends: the concierge. She guards the building, distributes the mail, cleans the staircases, corridors and lifts, and takes out the rubbish. But she is also the 'ears and eyes' of the building, and always knows everybody's business. A good concierge will be able to help you find your way around your neighbourhood.

Don't forget her Christmas tip each year (see above), or risk the consequences if you do! Concierges are a dying breed in Paris, but are generally liked by the inhabitants and owners of apartments. It is a good idea to warn the concierge when you are going away so that she can keep an eye on your apartment, and if necessary store your mail for you until you return.

MEETING PEOPLE

Moving to a new country is not only exciting and challenging, but also sometimes disorientating and a little frightening. This can especially be the case for the families and partners of those who have been transferred to work abroad. Finding friends with whom you can explore your new culture is vitally important to a rapid and happy adjustment to life in France.

The Regional Directory at the end of this book will help you to make contact with services and organisations for foreign residents across France. It will also help to familiarise you with the area to which you are moving. Do not be shy of contacting the organisations mentioned in the Directory. They exist to support you and help you to integrate rapidly with your new French friends and neighbours.

Places of worship

If you wish to practise your faith in English whilst living in France, there are many opportunities for you to do so. Most places of worship also serve as community centres, and you will find details of many events, services and clubs there.

A leaflet is available from the Gibraltar Diocesan Office, 14 Tufton Street, London SW1 giving details of more than 30 Church of England chaplaincies throughout France.

CHECKLIST

1. What efforts are you making to learn the language?

2. What efforts are you making to meet people?

3. Have you obtained your residence permit?

4
Finding Accommodation

This chapter offers a broad outline of the issues involved in renting and buying property in France. If you are buying property in France, you must take professional advice regarding your obligations as well as possible advantages. You should also refer to *How to Rent & Buy Property in France* by Clive Kristen.

DECIDING WHERE TO LIVE

For most people, the decision as to where to live in France will be governed by professional, family or educational obligations. But deciding what sort of accommodation to live in, whether to buy or rent, and in which area of the town or city, are largely personal choices. Think carefully about the following points when you decide where to live:

- **Size** – Do you prefer to have a larger home in a less popular but cheaper area, or a smaller home in a more central and/or expensive area?

- **Facilities** – Which facilities do you want to be nearest? Shops, schools, entertainment, your workplace?

- **Transport** – What public transport facilities are there nearby? Do you need parking space?

- **Safety** – How safe is the area you have chosen? Is it really as safe – or as dangerous – as you have been told?

If you have the opportunity it is a good idea to visit briefly the **quartier** (district) where you are considering living. Bear in mind the points above, be observant when you visit the *quartier*, and decide on your priorities before making a decision. Moving is expensive, time-consuming and unsettling.

RENTING PROPERTY

Understanding the adverts

To find accommodation in France, ask at your local newspaper kiosk or shop which newspapers contain the most advertisements in your area. Obviously you can use Estate Agencies (**Agents immobilier**), but there will be a charge to pay for their services. As a foreigner in France, you may well find it easier to deal directly with landlords rather than use agencies.

Above all you need to understand the terms and shorthand used in property advertisements so that you can concentrate on looking for the style of home which suits you and your budget. The examples given below will help you understand the jargon, and save you much valuable time.

*14e Studio **meublé**, salle d'eau. Près Montparnasse. 2.500 F / mois + charges. Tél. après 20h00.*

Furnished studio in the 14th arrondissement of Paris. Includes a 'bathroom' (probably) consisting of shower, washbasin and WC. Near to Montparnasse station. 2.500 FF per month plus building charges. Telephone the following number after 8pm.

Comment: This is probably a very small studio flat of about 18–20m^2. Much important information is missing. When you telephone to enquire about such studios ask about: the size of the flat; on which floor it is situated; if there is a lift; what the kitchen facilities are; what furnishings are provided; how much the building charges are (i.e. how much is the total rent). If there is no mention that it is furnished (**meublé**), then you must assume that there is no furniture at all.

This may also be one or possibly two **chambres de bonne** (maid's rooms) knocked into one flat. These are small rooms in the attics of large residential buildings. Single *chambres de bonne* are often let to students, but you sometimes have to share a WC and shower with other residents on the corridor.

3e Beaubourg. Immeuble ancien renové. Digicode, interphone. Studio 35m^2; neuf, aménagement standing. Séjour avec 2 fenêtres, poutres apparentes, cuisine équipée, salle de bains, wc, rangements. Libre 31/12 4.100 /mois charges comprises.

(Unfurnished) studio 35m^2 in the 3rd arrondissement of Paris, in the Beaubourg quartier, in an old building which has been restored with both Door Code and Inter-Phone. Newly redecorated to a good level. (Principal) living room with two windows, exposed beams, equipped kitchen, bathroom, WC, and built-in cupboards. Available from 31 December. 4.100 FF per month including building charges.

Comment: This is a much clearer advertisement. You still need to check about which floor the studio is on as it could well be 6th floor without a lift. Space is at a premium in French flats, and so it is important to know that there are built-in cupboards. Other terms for these are **placards** and **penderies** (normally referring to small built-in wardrobes). Check what is included in the kitchen area.

15e Convention. Immeuble pierre de taille, 2 pièces, 41m^2, clair, exposé sud. Fenêtre dans chaque piéce. Calme. Au 4e sans ascenseur. Digicode. Entrée, salle de bains (baignoire), wc, branchement lave-linge, séjour, coin-cuisine, chambre.

(Unfurnished) 2-room flat in the 15th arrondissement of Paris near Convention métro. Two rooms totalling 31m^2. South facing with a window in each room. Quiet, situated on the 4th floor without a lift. Door code. Entrance hall/passage, bathroom (with bath), WC, outlet for a washing machine, sitting room with 'kitchen corner', and bedroom.

Comment: This is a classic one-bedroom flat. The **Digicode** refers to the means of access to the building from the street. There may also be an inter-phone system as in the example above. The 'kitchen corner' is a classic feature of smaller flats. You will also see references to a **cuisine americaine**. This is a kitchen with a bar to separate it from the main room. **Pierre de taille** indicates that this is a good-quality stone building, probably well-maintained.

CLAMART (92) Maison 4 pièces, 80m^2, sur terrain 272m^2. Cuisine aménagée, salle de douche, wc séparées. Près commerces, écoles et transports. Dans quartier résidentiel calme. Chauffage gaz.

4-roomed house in Clamart in the Département Number 92, 80m^2 of a total property site of 272m^2. Fitted kitchen, shower room, separate WC. Near to shops, schools and transport. In a quiet residential area. Gas heating.

Comment: The number of rooms (two or more) does not normally include the entrance hall, WC or bathroom. In this case, there will be a sitting room, at least two bedrooms, and either a significant kitchen, or a dining room, or a third bedroom. The total property site probably includes a garden and parking space. It is a small house, but the advertiser is obviously seeking to attract a young couple with a small family. Note the facilities on offer.

Other points to note

Heating (**chauffage**) is either **individuel**, i.e. you control and pay for this yourself, or **collective**, in which case it is included in the building charges. However, in this case it is switched on and off at a defined date which may not always suit you. Air-conditioned residential property is almost unheard of.

Houses may have attics, but few if any flats will. However, certain flats will include the use of an individual cellar (**cave**). You should check the security and state of the cellar before deciding whether to use it to store your belongings. Large flats may have a **chambre de bonne** attached several floors above, although many chambres are now rented out separately.

Some flats may also have a parking space attached to them. This will instantly increase the price of the flat, especially in cities and large towns. Check whether the **parking** is in an attached car park, or a garage complex under the building. *Parkings* can also be separately rented if needed.

Viewing property

Select the properties which interest you, and call the numbers quickly to arrange to view them. If you are careful, you should be able to view several in one day, and so compare the properties more easily. In some cases the advertisements will simply announce a date, time and address to which you should come in order to visit. Expect to queue, and get there early.

Remember that when you go to view a property, you yourself are being viewed by the landlord as a prospective tenant. Competition is sharp for good homes, so you must be prepared.

● **Appear friendly and professional** – Smile and dress smartly. Nobody wants a difficult tenant, and a landlord will want to feel sure that you can pay the rent.

- **Take proof of your spending power** – Money talks loudly. Take along as many recent wage slips as you can, and also bank statements. They will almost certainly be asked for by the landlord. If you refuse to show them, it is very unlikely you will be accepted as a tenant.

- **Have your cheque book ready** to make a down payment on a rental if you and the landlord agree terms. However, **BE CAREFUL** to ask for a receipt from the landlord, and preferably your signed rental contract.

Questions the landlord will ask you
Expect to be asked at least one of the following questions by a prospective landlord:

- If you are employed, **'Do you have a permanent contract?'** If you have just arrived, take along past pay-slips, and an **attestation d'emploi** from your employer, stating that you have an indefinite contract, and your annual or monthly salary before tax.

- If you are a student, **'Do you have a carte d'étudiant?'** Renting to students is advantageous in one sense as there are tax benefits for landlords.

- **'Are you sure that you can afford the rent?'** Officially your monthly salary after tax and social security deductions must be three times the total rent on your home. In practice, this is rarely the case. However, it can be a sticking point, and with good reason. You should not over-stretch yourself financially.

- **'What guarantees can you offer for the payment of the rent?'** Very frequently landlords will ask for **références serieuses** and **garanties parentales**. This is a written undertaking either by your parents, or by your employer in some cases, that if you default on the rent, they will settle any outstanding debts. It is not an undertaking to be made lightly, as the standard notice period for leaving a French rental arrangement is three months.

  Students will almost certainly be asked for references and guarantors, but so too will young people who are in full-time employment (single or married). Foreigners are especially singled out for this treatment. Gentle negotiation and reassurance with an individual landlord can often resolve the problem, however.

Taking out a lease

Once you have chosen the property which interests you and been accepted for the tenancy, you will have to sign the lease (**contrat de location**). This should usually be a standard grey and green form, including mention of the laws governing rental agreements. They can be obtained from Tissot, 19 rue Lagrange, 75005 Paris. The front and back will be filled in and signed by your landlord and yourself, and the inside pages will include the general terms of the agreement. Two identical copies of the contract are signed and completed, one for you and one for the landlord.

Beware of 'home-made' contracts which could lead to difficult situations should a problem arise. They will certainly not offer you the same legal protection and security of residence as the formal contracts. Some landlords may have had a separate contract prepared by a lawyer for larger properties. Read contracts carefully before signing them, and if necessary seek professional advice. **Do not panic and never 'lease' a property without a contract (i.e. cash-in-hand).**

To conclude the contract, take along copies of your carte de séjour and passport, and your deposit (**caution**) for the flat. This sum is normally equivalent to two months' rent, but must be defined and mentioned in the contract. Normally the first month's rent is also paid in advance, making a total of three months' rent in advance.

The contract should include the name of the landlord; your name; the full address of your flat including the staircase, etc.; a description of the property; the length of the contract; the rent you are to pay, including building charges; when you are to pay it; and the amount of the *caution* you have paid for the property.

Etat des lieux

The contract is not completed until one final process has taken place known as the **état des lieux**. This should happen *before* you move in, and is undertaken with the landlord (or his representative) to establish the exact state of the property (e.g. cracks in the wall, broken windows, etc.).

Both of you keep a signed copy. Keep this safely in case your landlord later tries to make you pay for repairs which are not your fault. For furnished lets, you should also have an itemised inventory of the furnishings provided.

Additional costs when renting property

In addition to the caution and first month's rent, you may also find yourself presented with a bill for the **Frais** or **Honoraires** as they are sometimes called. These will be the costs involved in preparing a contract, and undertaking the *état des lieux*. A landlord is within his rights to use a bailiff (**huissier**) to undertake the *état des lieux*. All these charges will be at the tenant's expense.

The other additional cost you may face will be the estate agent's fee if you have used their services. This is also normally equivalent to one month's rent. Remember to check this before you take advantage of their services and include it in your budget.

Understanding your responsibilities as tenant
The general conditions of the standard contract list 16 responsibilities! The most important are:

1.   Paying the agreed rent at the agreed time (normally the first day of each month).

2.   Using the premises in a calm and reasonable manner for the purposes for which they were intended. Also not transforming them for another 'purpose' e.g. offices.

3.   Taking out a standard insurance policy against fire, water damage, etc.

4.   Obeying the regulations governing the day-to-day running of the building and concerning the **parties communes** (e.g. lifts, corridors, etc). These rules are agreed by all the owners (**copropriété**).

5.   Not sub-letting your property without prior written approval from your landlord.

6.   Carrying out day-to-day minor repairs.

The landlord's responsibilities
1.   Ensuring that the property is clean, that all repairs have taken place, and that all appliances included under the contract are in working order when the tenant enters the property.

2.   Ensuring that the tenant can 'peacefully enjoy' the use of the property. Should you find yourself with noisy neighbours or a problem elsewhere in the building, this will be important.

3.   Undertaking major repairs which are not the responsibility of the tenant.

4.   Not opposing improvements to the property which will not

change the basic use and structure of the property.

5. Sending a receipt for the monthly rent as and when demanded, and in the case of part-payments.

SHARING PROPERTY

In the case of a formal property share, for example two or more friends or an unmarried couple, it is best to arrange a separate formal lease between the landlord and each tenant in their own name dividing the rent between the tenants. Should one party then leave, the others will not be responsible for the rent of the person who has left.

It is also a good idea to put the electricity bill in the name of one tenant, and the telephone bill in the name of another. This provides each person with another proof of residence (**justifactif de domicile**), and helps to ensure each person's rights should a problem arise.

In the case of an informal flat share (i.e. sub-letting a room in a flat or house without a written contract – which is strictly illegal), you may be asked to pay a smaller caution (e.g. one month instead of two). But you should still **be sure to ask for a receipt from the person to whom you pay the caution**. Your rights in this situation are much less well-defined, so do be careful.

The French often say they do not like sharing with other French people as they are not good co-tenants! If you share a flat with a French person because you want to improve your French, remember the 'other side' may also wish to improve their English. Think carefully before entering into a flat-share and try to protect yourself as much as possible.

BUYING PROPERTY

If you decide to buy property in France, either as your principal home, or as a second home, the basic process is the same in both cases as regards the contracts you will have to sign and the charges you will have to pay.

Owning property in France
The distinction between 'freehold' and 'leasehold' does not exist in French property law. Instead, a distinction is drawn between co-ownership and free-standing property.

- Co-ownership means that the property (normally an apartment block) is divided into units. Each unit has a private area and a proportion of the communal area. The co-ownership regulations are known as **Le Réglement de Copropriété**. These regulations govern boundaries between private and communal areas, conditions for use of the building, etc. An assembly of the co-owners, the **Syndicat de Copropriétaires**, decides on changes to the regulations, and any major building works. The costs of any such works are divided amongst the co-owners.

- If you are buying your property independently, e.g. you are buying a house with a garden, you will have all the rights of ownership.

In either case, your purchase will be subject to the complicated French succession laws, and you should discuss these with your French legal advisers when you are planning your purchase.

Signing the contracts
When you and the seller have reached an agreement, there is a choice of two kinds of pre-contractual agreements which are possible:

1. **Promesse de vente** – This is a unilateral agreement to sell, signed by both the seller and buyer. Under the terms of such an agreement, the seller agrees to sell you the property by a certain time, for a set price, and according to set conditions. The buyer is allowed time to reflect on his decision, but must nonetheless pay a deposit, normally about 10 per cent of the full price.

    The advantage of this kind of agreement, which is very common, is that the seller cannot withdraw his or her acceptance of your offer if all the conditions of the agreement are met. The disadvantage is that if you as the buyer withdraw from the agreement, you lose your deposit.

2. **Compromis de vente** – Once again, both sides commit themselves to a change in ownership of the property. However, certain 'way out' clauses can be included in the agreement which are known as **conditions suspensives**. These conditions might include the granting of a mortgage (for which you normally have 40 days), or a town planning report (**certificat d'urbanisme**) etc. All these clauses must be adhered to, or you are entitled to cancel the agreement and reclaim your 10 per cent deposit.

Once the **notaire** (see below) has all the necessary information, a **projet de l'acte** (draft contract) can be produced. Copies are sent to the buyer and the seller for approval before the final contract is drawn up.

The **Acte Authentique de Vente** is the conveyancing agreement between the two parties. It will reiterate clauses from this pre-contractual arrangement, and will also clarify any further details. The following information must appear in the *acte*:

- identification of both parties concerned
- identification of the property in precise terms and the title of the property (**origine de propriété**)
- the date when you as the new owner will take possession of the property and be entitled to use it (**propriété de jouissance**)
- a **certificat d'urbanisme** which restates any town planning regulations affecting the property, as discovered by the notaire
- any guarantees and estimates.

The notaire retains the original contract, and copies are given to the buyer and seller, known as **l'expédition**. Once the sale has been registered at the **Bureau des Hypothéques**, no one else has any claim over the building. Finally the relevant section of the title deed is sent to the Land Registry.

Surveying your property

Structural surveys are not common practice in France as in the UK. Stringent building and construction regulations mean that there is usually no need. The seller, or in the case of a new house being built the construction company, are obliged to issue guarantees on the property. Builders must also be insured for work undertaken for ten years thereafter, and even in case of bankruptcy.

The notaire can include details of any guarantees on the property and a list of builders involved in your final agreement. A notaire or estate agent can carry out a simple survey if required. Otherwise, an **expert géometre** can check the total surface area of your new property, or you can arrange for a survey by an architect.

A new law in France concerning the sale of apartments requires the seller to state precisely the number of square metres of the total surface area of the apartment. Failure to do so can and does lead to prosecution. Prices normally include a calculation on the basis of square metres for apartments.

USING THE PROFESSIONALS

Le notaire

According to French law, every property transaction in France must be overseen by a notaire. The distinction in the French legal profession is between **avocats** who can appear in the courts (rather like barristers in the UK) and **notaires** who undertake contractual work rather like solicitors in the UK (such as conveyancing and the writing of wills).

Notaires must be impartial between the two parties of a property sale and are responsible for legally validating the deeds involved, advising clients and drawing up the necessary contracts. He or she can and does also sometimes act as a tax consultant, and also as an estate agent in certain cases.

The notaire is entitled to a legally determined sum as commission when acting as a sale negotiator. Normally this is around 10 per cent of the purchase price. If the building is a new property the notaire's fee is reduced to no more than 3 per cent (as an aid to the French construction industry). A building less than five years old which has never been occupied since construction also qualifies for this reduction in the notaire's fee.

Notaire's fees **(frais)** will eventually include money paid on your behalf, taxes, and dues and contingency duties. Overall costs are high but vary from region to region within a set scale, and depending on the type and value of the property.

The notaire's responsibilities when acting as intermediary for a sale are:

1. Verification of the seller including his/her right to sell the property.

2. Obtaining the relevant Land Registry papers, showing any planning objections to the property.

3. Contacting anyone with pre-emption rights to the property, and determining whether they plan to exercise these rights.

4. Contacting the **Conservation des Hypothéques** (mortgage/Land Registry) which must issue an **état hors formalité**. This shows any mortgages, securities, etc. on the property. Such debts must be payable and lower than the sale price to avoid redemption proceedings.

If you pay for the property through the notaire, s/he can withhold payment if it is discovered that the seller has used the property as collateral on a loan, until a **negative état sur formalité** has been issued.

The estate agent (agent immobilier)

About half of all property transactions in France are dealt with by estate agents. An estate agent cannot enter into negotiations unless s/he holds a **Mandat de Vente** (written power of attorney for sale) from the seller, or a **Mandat de Recherche** (written power of attorney to make a search) from you as the purchaser.

The seller usually has to pay the estate agent's commission, fixed by power of attorney, upon written completion of the transaction. Anything not referred to in the power of attorney cannot be charged by estate agents. They may fix the amount of commission they receive, but their scale of charges must be on open display. The commission must also represent a percentage of the purchase price. The price displayed for a property must include the commission.

FINANCIAL CONSIDERATIONS

Understanding the taxes payable

When setting up home in France, you will be liable for the following French taxes:

- **Government registration tax**. This tax is payable when you are completing your purchase, and when added to the fees of the notaire amounts to about 11 per cent of the property's purchase price.

  You will also be required to pay the equivalent of UK Land Registry fees and Stamp Duty. The rates depend on the size of the property and its grounds, the type of buildings on the land, and the age of the property. Once you have bought property in France, it must be registered with the tax authorities. If it is a secondary residence, contact the **Centre des Impôts des Non-résidents**. Tax-registration should take place before 30 April of any year.

- **Taxe foncière**. This is a local tax levied by the commune in which your new property is situated, and levied on you as the owner. Your name will be added to a register at the local mairie. The register comprises lists of owners, tax rates paid, and notional letting values of the property concerned.

- **Taxe d'habitation**. This local tax is not necessarily payable by the owner of the property, but by its occupant. If you rent a property you will normally be liable for this tax. The rate of tax payable is determined by the building's amenities and size. The basic rate is calculated according to the nominal letting value of property in the local area.

Insuring your property

You are required by French law to take out third-party insurance as soon as you move into your accommodation, or as soon as work has begun on your future home if it is still being built. This is known as **Civil Propriétaire**.

It is also highly advisable to take out insurance against fire, theft, etc. Comprehensive policies known as **assurances multirisques** are available, as are specific policies. The sum insured should reflect your insurable interest or potential loss according to the contract arranged. Co-owners should already be insured for the building itself and all communal areas. In addition you need to take out insurance on your own belongings.

Financing your purchase

Your own personal situation will determine the range of options open to you for financing your property purchase in France. Within France, the most common method of obtaining a mortgage is to apply to a high-street bank. A French bank will calculate the amount of money available for your mortgage according to your cash flow. A mortgage should be granted as long as your outgoings plus your mortgage repayments equal less than 30 per cent of your pre-tax income.

Successive French governments in recent years have tried to boost the property market by permitting loans at very low rates. It is worth enquiring widely about the possibilities before taking a decision.

HOUSING BENEFITS

The **caisse d'allocations familiales** administers three different housing benefits for those with limited resources. You cannot receive more than one of these benefits at any given time, and your right to access any of the benefits will almost certainly depend upon the length of time you have lived and worked in France. All the benefits are means-tested.

- **L'aide personalisée au logement (APL)** – This never covers the total amount of your housing expenses but only one part. It is available to owner-occupiers who have undertaken to improve their property under certain conditions, and also to tenants. For owner-occupiers, the benefit is generally paid directly to your loan agency or bank, whilst for tenants the benefit is normally paid direct to your landlord. In both cases the sum is deducted from your loan or rent.

- **L'allocation de logement familiale** and **l'allocation de logement sociale** – These benefits are available to tenants in a wide range of situations.
  - If you are already receiving another family benefit
  - or you have a child under 20 years old living at home
  - or you have been married for less than five years and have no children
  - or you are looking after a relative over 65 years of age or unable to work

  then you may be eligible for this benefit, depending upon your resources. A moving allowance is also available for those with limited resources. Applications should be made for this at your new *caisse d'allocations familiales* when you move.

Three other benefits also exist for those who undertake major structural work in their new homes. These are:

- **Le prêt à l'amélioration de l'habitat** – This is available to both owner-occupiers and tenants. This loan at a rate of 1 per cent is available for necessary improvements, such as heating or sanitary conditions. It is not means-tested, but you must already qualify for another family benefit. The loan is currently limited to 7,000 FF, and 80 per cent of the total cost of the works. Repayments take place over 36 months. For more details, you should contact your local *caisse d'allocations familiales*.

- **Assistance from ANAH (Agence Nationale pour l'Amélioration de l'Habitat)** – This is not means-tested. Basically it applies to vacant buildings more than 15 years old which are being made habitable. Normally it is paid only to owners, who commit to renting the property afterwards. Generally the benefit is around 25 per cent of the total cost of the agreed works, but can be higher. To find out more contact the ANAH at the local *direction départementale de l'équipement*.

● **La prime à l'amélioration de l'habitat** – A means-tested 'bonus' available to owner-occupiers which varies from region to region. **This benefit is of particular interest to those adapting homes for people with handicaps or disabilities**, amongst other more common measures regarding health and hygiene. The total amount of the bonus cannot exceed 20 per cent of the real costs of the works, within a limit of 70,000 FF.

However, this bonus can also be added to another bonus worth 50 per cent of the works necessary to allow access, or conversion for use by, handicapped people. The limit on this second bonus is 20,000 FF. Hence for such works costing a total of 110,000 FF, it is possible to be awarded state assistance totalling 34,000 FF.

Applications for the *prime de l'amélioration de l'habitat* should be made to the *section habitat* of the *direction départementale de l'équipement* (except in Paris where applications should be made to the *préfecture*).

MAKING CONNECTIONS

Electricity and gas

Probably the easiest way to deal with gas and electricity contracts (administered by the state-run EDF-GDF company which has a monopoly) is to take over the contracts of the previous residents of your property, be it rented or purchased. Contact your local EDF agency to arrange to have the meter read before you take possession of the property, or to establish a new contract if necessary.

Bills normally arrive quarterly, and can be paid at the post office using a **mandat** (postal order), or by cheque sent by post. Notices regarding meter readings will be sent to you or posted in your building. You must ensure access on the day of the reading. Normally concierges are willing to help if you live in an apartment and cannot be present.

Collective (central) heating is controlled by the date not the temperature. Normally it is turned on in October and turned off in April. In smaller and older properties, you may well find that it is necessary to install extra electric heaters.

Water

As with electricity and gas, it is probably easiest to take over existing contracts when you purchase a new property. Tenants normally have their water charges included in the general charges they pay with their rent. Water is supplied by private companies. Arrange for a reading of the water meter when taking over a contract. Bills arrive about every three months.

Telephone

In 1998, France Télécom lost its national monopoly in France. However, in reality you still need to take out a France Télécom contract for line rental. The former state operator is now locked in price battles with its competitors – currently Cegetel and Bouygues Télécom (in the autumn of 1998). You will need to contact each operator to discuss the offers available.

At the time of writing, Cegetel offers more interesting rates for long-distance calls and international calls, especially to the UK (as they are partnered by British Telecom). If you take out a Cegetel line subscription (**abonnement**), you simply dial 7 instead of dialling 0 at the start of the number.

Television

When you buy or rent a television in France, the shop from which you purchase or rent the machine will automatically send your name and address to the TV licence office (**Centre de Rédevance Audiovisuel**). They will then in turn send you an annual bill, normally around January or February each year. You only have to pay a licence fee for one TV per household, so if you buy a second TV for the bedroom or the kitchen, it will be covered under the first licence.

DEALING WITH PROBLEMS

Structural problems

If you are the cause of a problem, such as a leak or a short-circuit, you are obviously responsible for repairing the damage or the problem. Contact your insurance company rapidly in order to establish what help they can offer you in the case of a major problem.

Tenants who are the victims of such problems should inform their landlords immediately. Landlords often have their own plumbers and electricians who deal with such problems for them, and send the bills directly to them. If you cannot contact your landlord, and the situation is an emergency, you will have to arrange and pay for action yourself. Keep copies of the bill, and send the original bills to your landlord for reimbursement once you have explained the situation to him/her.

The Syndic of your building will have the names of companies they use in such situations, and whom they can recommend to you. But it is a good idea to try and arrange at least one other estimate in order to keep the costs involved at a minimum. You should note that calling out an electrician or plumber for an immediate visit or at the weekend will normally prove expensive.

Insects, pests and vermin

Unfortunately these may affect you no matter where you live. Your local **mairie** will very often have a department which deals with insect problems such as wasp nests or cockroaches. Call to find out about this service, and check how much it costs. It is not too expensive, and can save a great deal of unpleasant trouble.

Cockroaches unfortunately tend to appear in clean homes as well as dirty ones, mainly due to the fact that you have unknowingly brought home their eggs on the under-side of packets bought in supermarkets! There are plenty of sprays and traps available for ridding yourself of this problem. Major infestations should be dealt with by professionals.

Vermin can also be dealt with by using traps and poison readily available in high-street shops. However, you obviously need to be careful about using these methods if you have children or pets. Try and locate the mouse-hole, place poison inside the hole, and seal it.

Regular disinfections should take place of your entire building organised by the Syndic. Be careful to note when these are to happen, and arrange for access to your flat even if you do not have a problem. All flats in a building need to be disinfected for the process to be really effective. If you have a problem with vermin, warn your landlord and the Syndic so that they can arrange for these measures to be taken.

Problem neighbours

Dealing with problem neighbours is often difficult and unpleasant. In the first instance, you need to try and speak to them about whatever is the source of the problem, be it noise or a leak. Try and remain calm and reasonable, even if your neighbours appear to be the opposite. In the end, your own self-control will work in your favour.

If the problems persist, you will obviously need to speak to them once again. Keep a careful note of when you spoke to them, and a brief record of your conversations. Tenants with persistent problems are fully entitled to contact your landlord for help since he/she is obliged to ensure that you can 'peacefully enjoy' the use of the property you are renting.

Eventually putting your complaints in writing is a useful way of proving you have tried to resolve the situation. Keep a copy of the letter and place the original in your neighbour's post box. Sending a registered letter of complaint with proof of delivery (**lettre recommandé avec avis de récéption**) is an elaborate but sure way of proving you have complained.

The final resort for dealing with neighbours depends on whether they are tenants or owner-occupiers.

- **Tenants** – Speak to the concierge and find out the name of their landlord. You may need to ask your own landlord to help you to find his/her address. If a landlord receives repeated complaints about tenants, they may be forced to leave the property.

- **Owner-occupiers** – This is a more difficult situation. Ultimately you would need to have a petition signed by the other residents of the building (many of whom will probably refuse even if they are sympathetic) before any definite action could be taken.

In both cases, the police can be asked to intervene. By law, excessive noise before 08h00 and after 22h00 is not permitted. If you own your property in an apartment block, you can also contact the Syndic of the building for advice and help.

CHANGING YOUR ADDRESS

Moving homes in France is not simply a case of finding and securing your new address, and then informing your family and friends where to find you. A great many other people and organisations, listed below, must also be informed.

Moving home action plan
1. **Landlords** – Be careful to respect the notice periods stipulated in your rental agreements.

2. **Electricity and gas** – Contact your current EDF agency ten days before you move to have your meter read. The cost of

terminating your current contract will be sent to your new address. At the same time, contact your new agency to establish the new contract or arrange to take over the existing contract.

3. **Water** – as above.

4. **Telephone** – Contact your current and future France Télécom agencies. Arrange termination of your existing contract about eight days before the move. In certain cases if you are staying within the same exchange area, you can keep the same number if you wish. A recorded message can also be arranged on the old number for three months informing callers of your new number.

5. **Post** – Organise a **faire-suivre** at the post office for all your post. This should be done no later than five days before the move. In April 1998 the forwarding service for one year cost 110 FF. Generally it works well. However, you might wish to consider tipping your current concierge to check that any post does actually reach the new address.

6. **Carte de séjour and passport** – After you have moved, the new address must appear on your official documents.

7. **Driving licence, carte grise and car registration** – You have one month in which to accomplish the change of address on your carte grise. If you change départements, your car must also be re-registered.

8. **Insurance policies** – You will need to inform your insurance companies of a change of address. You can either terminate your existing house insurance, or transfer it to your new residence. This may cost more or less depending on whether your new home is smaller or larger than before.

9. **Social security** – Fifteen working days before you move, contact your current and future *caisse d'assurance maladie* to arrange for your new card(s), and the transfer of your files. This is not the most efficient or speedy of services, so allow plenty of time....

10. **ANPE** – If you are registered at the local job centre, inform your old centre of your forthcoming change of address. Visit your new centre as soon as possible after moving in.

11. **Family benefits** – Inform your local *caisse d'allocations familiales* of your intended move 15 working days before the date. They should contact your new caisse for you.

12. **Bank** – Inform the bank of your change of address as soon as possible. This will allow them not only to send correspondence to the correct address, but also to print new cheque books for you. You may also wish to change branches.

13. **Tax offices** – Admittedly, they were probably not on your mailing list for change of address cards. However, they have a nasty habit of finding out where you are in any case.
    Inform your current tax office before you move of your change of address. The following year, you will send your tax declaration to your old tax office, but marked with your new address on the first page. You must also inform the TV licence centre of your change of address. **Correspondence from tax offices is *not* forwarded by the post office, but sent back to the senders. This can have serious consequences.**

14. **Municipal crêches** – You must enrol your children at your future mairie as soon as possible. You must also respect the one-month notice period for withdrawing your children from their current crêche.

15. **Primary schools** – Before moving, ask the school for a **certificat de radiation**. (This does not mean that your child glows in the dark, but that s/he has been struck off the school register.) At the same time, contact the schools office of your new mairie to arrange an appointment. The will inform you which school catchment area you now fall under.

16. **Collège or lycée** – Before moving ask the school director for a **certificat de sortie** for your children. The appropriate files should then be transferred directly to the new school.

17. When you have completed all of the above, sit down, pour yourself a large drink, and swear never to move home again in France...!

5
Working in France

This chapter offers a general guide on working in France. For more detailed information, you should refer to *How to Get a Job in France* by Mark Hempshell.

Finding work in France at the moment is far from easy, with unemployment at about 12 per cent. You need to prepare yourself as best you can in advance – certainly in terms of language – to succeed in finding employment once you arrive. It remains to be seen if the 30 per cent rise in the value of the French Stock Market in 1997–98 translates into renewed employment opportunities.

Nationally, the general trend is towards a development of the tertiary (service industry) sector, which employed 65 per cent of private sector employees in 1997 (source: *L'Expansion*, 4–18 December 1997). The same year saw a significant rise in the number of jobs in tourism and leisure-related industries; unskilled work in supermarkets and hypermarkets, cleaning and security work, etc., including as a result new jobs for managers; and jobs in information technology, advertising and management services.

Overall, the most dynamic area for job creation in 1997 was rural Brittany, where not only tourism but also telecommunications have created jobs. The Seine-et-Marne region to the south of Paris (home to EuroDisney), and the Vienne region around Poitiers in the west (home to the theme park Futuroscope) have seen significant job creation at and around their leisure attractions. However, the number of jobs created is still way below the number of job seekers.

Paris ranked last of all in the employment creation table of départements in France in 1997, with an unemployment rate of 12.6 per cent. Growth industries in 1997 were information technology with the arrival of the Euro and the year 2000, and the advertising sector. The Hauts-de-Seine and Yvelines regions bordering Paris on the west have benefited from the decentralisation of company headquarters.

The Hauts-de-Seine, including the business centre of La Défense, had the highest average wage in France of 171,600 FF in 1997, 50,000 FF more than the national average.

LOOKING FOR WORK

Looking for work is a full-time job in itself. In France, there are a variety of ways in which you can seek work.

Registering at a job centre

Probably the least useful is to register at the local state-run job centre, the **Agence Nationale Pour l'Emploi (ANPE)**. You must register in person, and written applications will not be accepted. Proof of permanent residence in France (your **carte de séjour**) will be required, and they may also ask to see your passport. Job advertisements are displayed in the centres, and workshops, counselling and personal interviews are available.

Using recruitment agencies

Although employers are obliged to inform the ANPE of vacancies in their companies, they are much more likely to seek the help of recruitment agencies (**conseils de recruitment**) and head-hunters (**chasseurs de têtes**) to fill vacancies. Most agencies are accessible only by appointment. You therefore need to prepare and send your CV and covering letter (see the section on applying for jobs later in this chapter) in order to open these doors.

There are now several agencies in Paris which specialise in bilingual appointments, particularly for secretarial and administrative work. Providing that you do have a good working knowledge of French, your greatest immediate asset in the search for work will be that you are English mother-tongue.

Responding to newspaper advertisements

The most important newspaper for job advertisements in France is *Le Figaro* every Monday. The separate '**économie**' section normally carries a wide variety of jobs of all levels and areas. These are repeated every Wednesday in the job newspaper *Carrières et Emplois*, which also includes jobs advertised in *Le Parisien*, and sometimes advertisements from *The International Herald Tribune*.

Le Monde on Mondays and Tuesdays carries a selection of well-paid jobs, and the business newspapers *Les Echos* and *La Tribune* also carry similar job advertisements. *Les Echos* has a reciprocal agreement with *The Financial Times*. This means that you may be able to start your job-search even before you move to France.

Libération also has a small but developing jobs section each Monday, and magazines such as *L'Express* and *Le Nouvel*

Observateur also carry a variety of job advertisements. Regional newspapers are also an important source of opportunities. In Paris, two free magazines (*France-USA Contacts* and *The Free Voice*) have significant job sections of interest to English-speakers.

Sending unsolicited job applications

The final approach to job-hunting in France is to send out unsolicited job applications (**candidatures spontanées**), composed of your CV and a general covering letter. This is an important method of filling vacancies in France, which fits in with the general 'networking' approach which is highly prevalent.

A well-presented CV and letter, followed up by a phone-call if appropriate, can secure you at least a first interview for a post that nobody else knew was even vacant.

REPLYING TO JOB ADVERTISEMENTS

Job advertisements come in a wide variety of shapes and word forms. Figure 5 contains a number of standard terms. The explanation given below will help you decode precisely what is being offered.

The basic format is to indicate the name of the company and/or its activity first, then to indicate the post that is being offered,

---

Importante société internationale de prêt-à-porter en plein expansion recherche

Vendeurs/Vendeuses confirmées

pour ses boutiques sur la Région Parisienne.

Jeune et dynamique, vous avez les sens du contact, une première expérience professionnelle réussite dans ce domaine, et vous cherchez maintenant à évoluer dans votre carrière.

Envoyez votre candidature (lettre, CV, photo et prétentions) à DRH, Wear-Well S.A., Service Recrutement, 19, rue Eugene Leblanc, 92300 Levallois-Perret, sous réf 24679.

Fig. 5. Sample job advertisement.

followed by a brief description of the candidate profile the company is seeking. It is important to understand this brief profile – no matter how standard or banal it may seem – in order to compose the correct application letter indicating your suitability for the job.

Two common specifications given in job advertisements are the level of education required of applicants, and whether the position is **cadre** or **non-cadre**. Both of these require explanation.

- **Bac + 3** or **Bac + 4** etc. – This indicates that graduates are being sought who have at least the level of **baccalauréat** (A-levels), plus three years of further education, or whatever number is indicated. Bac + 5, for instance, would require an initial higher education degree, plus perhaps a masters degree. A further specialised **cycle** may also be required for certain jobs. **Niveau bac** means A-level education is the minimum.

- **Cadre** – This is basically a senior executive post, unique to France. Advantages include better salaries (in general) and better social security benefits later in life, and a certain 'snob' value. Disadvantages include long hours for no extra pay. **Cadres** are not normally paid overtime, whereas it is obligatory for **non-cadres**.

Decoding the final part of the advertisement is crucial. For the sample advertisement in Figure 5, your complete application must include the following items:

- **Lettre d'accompagnement** – This **MUST** be handwritten in impeccable French, well-presented, and no more than one side of A4 paper. Standard forms of letter suitably adapted are perfectly acceptable, but typed letters will simply be ignored. Many firms in France still use graphology as a selection test for candidates, especially for more important jobs.

- **CV** – Your curriculum vitae (CV) or resumé must be neatly typed and easy-to-read, in the French format, and no more than one side of A4 paper. Make sure that you bring out the most important and relevant elements in your experience which suit you to the job for which you are applying. On average, most recruiters spend about one or two minutes reading what has taken hours to prepare. They need to see your suitability right away.

- **Salary/Prétentions** – Some advertisements clearly state salary, some give a salary range according to experience (e.g. 200–250 KF = 200,000–250,000 FF), and some advertisements ask for your **prétentions**, as in Figure 5. Basically, this is asking you to state what you are willing to accept as a salary – which is a tricky business!

You therefore need to know what the 'average' salary is for someone of your experience, and for such a position. Looking at similar advertisements can help. **Only include your prétentions if you are asked for them**, or in certain cases when you make a **candidature spontanée**. Otherwise, pretentions will have a much more English meaning!

- **Photo** Despite being the land of *liberté, égalité et fraternité*, the French still tend to pre-select their candidates to a large extent on a rather superficial basis. On the other hand, as in the case of our advertisement in Figure 5, appearance is important. As with **prétentions**, only send a photo when you are asked to do so.

  Do not use a photo taken in a photo booth at a railway station, etc. Go to a photo shop and arrange to have a set of four **black and white** passport-size photos taken in which you are dressed well and appropriately for the position for which you are applying. This should only cost about 40 FF, and is money well spent. One photo should then be stapled to the top right-hand corner of your CV.

Preparing your French CV

Preparing your French curriculum vitae (or resumé) can be heart-rending, especially if you have spent your university career 'collecting CV points'! You only have one side of A4 on which to cram in the information in a relevant, readable and eye-catching manner. There is therefore no point in telling potential employers how you captained a cricket team (which the French don't even understand), if it means sacrificing space.

Figure 6 shows you the basic format for preparing your CV. Any of the decent guides available in France will help you to choose one of the variations on this theme which best suits your experience. Contrary to popular opinion, there is no one 'correct' way to present a CV in France. But what is definitely wrong is to produce the kind of detailed CV common in the United Kingdom.

Points to remember are:

1.   Your **Etat Civil** (name, address, telephone numbers, marital status and number of children) always comes in a neat little

Paul Williams
75, rue Aristide Briant,
75019 Paris
Tél. 01 47 97 14 39 (Dom.)

Etat civil
Situation de famille: Célibataire
Nationalité: Britannique
Né le 15 mars 1969 à Bristol (Angleterre)

Formation
1987 – « A' Levels » (équivalent du baccalauréat) en géographie, français et histoire contemporain.
1991 – « Bachelor of Arts Honours Degree «, University of Warwick (Diplôme d'Histoire Contemporaine en 3 ans).

Langues
Anglais (langue maternelle)
Français (parlé et écrit couramment)

Expérience professionnelle
Depuis septembre 1996: Manager du département prêt-à-porter masculin auprès du Buyright Limited, Manchester, Angleterre.

– Responsable d'une équipe de cinque vendeurs dans un important magasin en plein coeur d'une des plus grandes villes d'Angleterre.
– Responsable de la commande des stocks.
– Participation à l'élaboration du plan général du management du magasin.

1994 – 1996: Assistant au directeur d'exportation auprès du Woolbridge Products Limited, Manchester, Angleterre.

- Réceptions et suivi des commandes (y compris les clients à l'étranger) et grande expérience du service facturation.

1992 – 1994: Vendeur, Woolbridge Products, Manchester, Angleterre.
1991 – 1992: Vendeur auprès du Riley Products, Sydney, Australie

Autres expériences
1987 – 1988: Voyages en divers pays de l'Afrique du sud.
1991 – 1992: Séjour en Australie et Nouvelle Zealand
1989 – 90: Président du « History Society « à l'Université de Warwick
Permis de conduire

Fig. 6. Sample French CV.

section at the top of the page. Leave space on the right-hand side for a photo if necessary.

2. Start with the most recent/current employment, and work backwards. Arguably you should adopt the same practice with your education.

3. Referees are not normally included on a French CV. They may be called for subsequently, but are not normally asked for in advance.

4. Companies and consultants receive thousands of CVs. To succeed, yours must stand out. Use a good quality paper, and if possible a similar envelope. Ask French friends to check your spelling, grammar and punctuation. The French are very picky indeed about such things.

Writing your application letter

Even if you have the perfect CV and are amply qualified for the job, you may well fall foul of a recruiter with a badly written or badly presented letter.

Standard form letters are acceptable. However, it is much better to take the standard form and adapt it to the job for which you are applying, bringing out the major points in favour of your application. The letter should not be simply a repetition of your CV. Figure 7 is an example of a typical **lettre d'accompagnement** in response to the advertisement in Figure 5.

Examples of standard letters can be found not only in CV guides, but also in many good French–English dictionaries, such as *Le Robert*.

Points to remember are:

1. The letter must never exceed one side of A4 paper.

2. Begin by stating that you are replying to the advertisement in *X* newspaper, and give the date of the advertisement. If a **réf.** (**référence**) is given in the advertisement, remember that it must appear in both the letter *and* on the envelope.

3. If the name of the person and their gender is not given, begin simply by '**Monsieur**'. Do not write '**Cher Monsieur**', as this would imply a degree of intimacy.

4. As with the CV, the letter must be impeccably written, on good quality stationery.

75 rue Aristide Briant
75019 Paris

Wear-Well S.A.
19, rue Eugene Leblanc
92300 Levallois Perret

Paris, le 3 avril 199X

Monsieur,

Votre offre d'emploi pour un poste de vendeur auprès du Wear-Well parue dans Le Figaro économie du 30 mars, (réf. 24679), m'a beaucoup intéressé.

De nationalité britannique, et doté d'une forte expérience du domaine de prêt-à-porter, je suis actuellement à la recherche d'un poste en France qui me permettrait d'évoluer dans ma vie professionnelle.

Vous trouverez dans le curriculum vitae ci-joint le détail de mes études et de mes activités professionnelles. Le montant de mes prétentions s'élève à 10 000 F brut par mois.

Je suis à votre disposition pour vous fournir toute information complémentaire. Dans l'attente d'un entretien à cet effet, je vous prie d'agréer, Monsieur, l'expression de mes salutations distingueés.

Paul Williams

P.J.: Curriculum vitae

Fig. 7. Sample French application letter.

5. Finish the letter with a standard formula. Generally, men assure their correspondents of their '**salutations distinguées**', whilst women send their '**sentiments distinguées**'.

Going to the interview

The same basic rules apply in France as anywhere else in the world. Dress appropriately and smartly, arrive in good time, shake hands on meeting your interviewer – and smile!

As a foreigner newly arrived in France, you can expect to be asked about your motivation for moving to France, as well as your experience. Prepare yourself as much in advance as possible for the questioning, as your language abilities will be under scrutiny. Allowances will be made for the fact that you are a foreigner, but you must understand at least 95 per cent of what is being talked about.

CONDITIONS OF EMPLOYMENT

Looking at employment contracts

The two basic forms of contract for legal employment in France are the fixed-term contract, and the indefinite contract. Similar basic contracts also exist for student placement workers (**stagiaires**), au pairs, and part-time (**temps partielle**) workers.

- **Contrats à durée déterminée (CDD)** – Fixed-term contracts. These can only be applied in certain circumstances, such as a sudden increase in business, or for seasonal work (e.g. at Christmas), or to cover pregnancy leave. They may not exceed nine months, but can be renewed a maximum of twice. After two renewals, the company is obliged to offer you a permanent contract. CDDs are increasingly common in France.

- **Contrats à durée indéterminée (CDI)** – Indefinite contracts. These are the most common form of contract in France. They are also the most preferable form of contract for foreigners moving to France, as they will provide you with longer-term residency rights. Remember that your **carte de séjour** will initially be limited to the length of your work contract.

There is no standard model for a contract in France, and surprisingly, there does not even have to be a written contract. However, the following points should normally appear in a written contract:

- name and address of both parties
- job title and description of duties
- place of work
- pay scale coefficient
- rate of pay and bonuses, etc.
- hours of work and holiday entitlement
- notice period required by either employer or employee.

Your contract will almost certainly include a trial period (**période d'essai**), lasting from one to three months. During this period, both you and your employer have the right to terminate your contract without notice. Your acceptance for a position is also subject to a general medical examination (**visite médicale**) by the independent firm doctor.

Salary

The minimum wage in France is usually known by the initials **SMIC** (which stand for **Salaire Minimum Interprofessionel de Croissance**). It is currently just over 6,000 FF per month. The SMIC is linked to the cost of living index, which is reviewed every six months. When this index rises by 2 per cent or more, the level of the SMIC is raised. Pay reviews must take place once a year by law. However, salaries above the SMIC do not have to be increased, even if the cost of living has increased.

Salaries are normally quoted in contracts as a total annual figure before social security deductions, but may also be quoted on a monthly or hourly basis. Salaries are usually paid monthly, on around the 26th day of each month. This is to allow the transfer of money into your account to settle bills due at the beginning of the month (notably rent). Payment is normally by standing order to your bank account, except for lower salaries which may be paid by cheque.

Bonuses

Most French firms offer bonuses of a thirteenth month's pay (**13ème mois**). This is normally paid as one lump sum at one point in the year, usually in December. Other companies offer profit-sharing schemes (**participation des salariés aux résultats de l'entreprise**), which is an obligation in companies with more than 100 employees. Both of these, and any similar benefits, are normally mentioned in your contract.

If you are employed under a CDD, you are entitled to an end of contract bonus (**indemnité de fin de contrat**). This is equivalent to 5 per cent of your salary, and in addition to any other bonuses.

Working hours

The legal working week is currently 39 hours in France, over a five-day period. In the year 2000, under legislation currently before the Assemblée Nationale, this will be cut to 35 hours per week. Your general working hours should be marked in your contract. The traditional long French lunch is rarer in Paris than the provinces. However, government offices still observe a total shutdown between 12h00 and 14h00.

Employees can be asked to work paid overtime hours, but cannot be forced to work more than a certain number of hours per year (currently 130). The present government intends to tax overtime hours more heavily to encourage employers to take on extra staff rather than paying existing staff for longer hours. Currently, overtime is paid at 25 per cent more per hour for the first eight hours, and 50 per cent more for every hour in addition to that.

Holiday entitlement and leave of absence

Holiday entitlement is gradually built up on the basis of 2.5 days per month worked, to a total of five weeks annual paid leave. This does not include public holidays. Normally this is taken in segments over the course of the year – one week in winter and spring, and a longer break in the summer months. Some companies still observe the traditional total shutdown in August, when seemingly the whole of France heads for the hills, the coast or the airports.

Any existing holiday arrangements are normally honoured when you join a company, but be careful to check this. The 'holiday calendar year' normally runs from 1 May to 30 April. Some companies allow you to carry over some holiday entitlement, but you must be careful not to lose holiday time not taken within the required period.

Extra days off are often allowed under the terms of **conventions collectives** (see below) for close family bereavements, weddings or moving house. Check this with your personnel department.

Food and travel

Many French firms offer either a luncheon voucher scheme (**ticket restaurant**), or a canteen facility. In Paris, the firm will normally reimburse half of the cost of your **carte orange** (travel pass) each month. This will be paid directly with your salary, and will be indicated on your pay slip (**bulletin de paie**).

Insurance and pensions
In addition to the regular contributions you will make to the state schemes, you will probably find deductions on your pay slips for complementary health insurance via the **mutuelle** to which the firm subscribes, and to a complementary pension scheme.

These contributions, if they are levied, are obligatory. However, they are very worthwhile, and will cover most if not all of the shortfall in state reimbursements for medical treatment. Ask your personnel department or your colleagues how to apply to the **mutuelle** for supplementary reimbursement.

Unemployment insurance (**allocation d'assurance chômage**) is automatically included in your social security contributions.

Collective agreements
Conventions collectives, as they are known, exist in many varied professions. They cover everything from compassionate leave to the right to union membership, as well as complementary health rights, loans and rates of pay. They may substantially alter the general conditions of work, and you should note if mention is made of a *convention* in your contract.

Professional training
French firms with more than ten employees are obliged to set aside 1.2 per cent of their gross annual payroll for **formation continue**. This may be used for advanced training, but also for basic language training. In both cases it could be of great interest to you. However, the allocation is entirely at the discretion of the employer.

Worker representation to the management
There are three levels of worker representation, all of which may apply in the same company. This depends upon the number of employees.

1. **Déléguées du personnel** (employee delegates) – Any company with more than ten employees must have déléguées, with the number of déléguées increasing in proportion to the size of the workforce. They present employee concerns to the management over individual and collective working conditions, job roles, wages, and application of employment laws.

2. **Comité d'entreprise** (works council) – Both the *déléguées du personnel* and the members of the *comité d'entreprise* are elected by the employees, by secret ballot, with representatives for the cadres and non-cadres in a company. There must be more than 50 employees on the payroll for a company to have a *comité d'entreprise*. The *comité* normally also includes a senior management member, and a member of the personnel department.

The *comité* discusses in more general terms the same concerns as the *déléguées*. However, it should also be informed of general firm policies before they are implemented, and is entitled to view the company accounts annually.

The *comité* normally has a budget of its own linked to the number of employees, which is used to enable employees and their families to undertake cultural and leisure pursuits at reduced rates. Find out about any such offers when you join your firm. You may also find that your *comité* has offers available on the purchase of new spectacles, etc.

3. **Union membership** – The presence of unions is most heavily felt in nationalised and heavy industry. It is rarer in the private sector, and under the terms of certain *conventions collectives*, simply not allowed. If union membership is allowed, the right to strike is guaranteed under French law (and freely exercised!), except for certain essential public employees.

Dealing with conflicts at work
If at all possible, it is best to try and contain a problem before it gets out of hand. Speak to the personnel department, and if they cannot or will not help, then try your *déléguée du personnel*.

Questions raised by the *déléguées* during their confidential meetings with the management are recorded and viewed annually by the Work Inspectors (**inspection du travail**), who have the right to pursue an enquiry if they think it necessary. This may also help you in more serious disciplinary cases, or worst of all, in the case of dismissal.

Companies are obliged by law to display the address of the nearest *inspection du travail*, and a telephone number. You can go to them for free confidential advice. You can also find their telephone numbers in the *Pages Jaunes*.

Dismissal
Firing someone in France is almost as difficult for the employer as it

is for the employee to find a job in the first place! Nonetheless, it does happen. Strict procedures must be followed, including written warnings. If the procedures are not adhered to, you have a strong case for compensation, especially if you have not been paid your full share of holiday pay, etc.

The two grounds for dismissal are **faute grave** (gross misconduct or incompetence), or economic, in which case you are entitled to 'first refusal' if your job is re-created subsequently. If you intend to contest your dismissal, you can take your employer to an industrial tribunal (**conseil des Prud'hommes**). Winning your case would entitle you to compensation but not reinstatement. Most companies prefer to settle out-of-court rather than face a public trial.

Legal aid does exist in France (**l'aide juridictionelle**) for those on low incomes (currently less than 7,353 FF per month), including the income of your spouse or partner. For further information, contact your local mairie.

SELF-EMPLOYMENT IN FRANCE

Being your own boss in France is not as easy – or as cheap – as you might think it ought to be. Nonetheless, in 1997 there were 500,000 self-employed people in France, representing 6 per cent of the workforce and producing more than 7 per cent of France's Gross Domestic Product.

Becoming either a **travailleur independent**, or a **professionel non salarié**, or a member of a **profession libéral**, (all of which are in fact the same thing), a **commerçant** (independent shopkeeper) or an **artisan** (i.e. a craftsman) involves certain basic and important steps at the outset to avoid pitfalls and nasty shocks.

Visiting the local tax office

This is not an obligation, but a wise precautionary measure. The tax inspector (**inspecteur des impôts**) will be able to tell you if you can open up your business as a self-employed person. He or she will also set out your financial obligations, including those for VAT (known as **TVA** in France).

Registering your new business

You must register your new business with the appropriate authorities, which is the **Union de Recouvrement des Cotisations de Sécurité Sociale et d'Allocations Familiales** – more commonly and easily known as **URSSAF**. To register your business, contact the local **Centre de Formalités des Entreprises (CFE)**. In Paris, the address is URSSAF, 3 rue Franklin, 93518 Montreuil cedex. Tel: 01 48 51 10 10 or 01 49 20 10 10. Fax: 01 49 20 22 04. To avoid paying excess social charges (which are very heavy in any case), the best time to register your new business is at the beginning of a quarterly period (e.g. 1 April). Once you have made the initial '**déclaration du début d'activité non salariée**' (un-waged activity), the CFE will automatically undertake the next steps for you, which are:

- The **déclaration d'existence** to the tax inspector, and the enrolment for the **taxe professionelle**.

- Your enrolment at the **caisse d'allocations familiales** (family allowance centre), run by URSSAF itself.

- Your enrolment at the **caisse d'assurance maladie des professions libérales** (local health authority for non-salaried professions). They will offer you a choice of compulsory medical insurance schemes, of which the largest is the Mutuelle de Mans, 18 rue de Londres, 75009 Paris. Tel: 01 40 16 72 72.

- Your enrolment at the **caisse d'assurance vieillesse** (for pensions). Most professions have their own individual *caisse*. However, if you do not fall into an established category, you will be enrolled at CIPAV, 21 rue de Berri, 75403 Paris Cedex 08. Tel: 01 45 68 28 90.

- Your registration at **INSEE** – INSEE is the national statistical office. Your registration here acts as a form of business registration, which will lead to your business receiving the necessary SIREN and SIRET numbers.

Registering for TVA at your local tax office
This is an optional step which you can take at the tax office. Companies will expect you to charge them TVA (VAT in England), and you will be able to reclaim TVA on purchases if you are registered. On the other hand, you are not obliged to charge TVA to individuals – hence you can be more competitive in your pricing policy.

Joining an 'association agréée'
This is another optional step to take, but very worthwhile. An **association agréée** not only offers advice and support, but can also offer an important reduction (**abattement fiscal**) in your tax burden. Conditions of membership are simply falling into one of the self-

employed categories, conforming to basic accounting rules, and paying an annual membership fee of around 1,000 FF.

This **abattement fiscal** is achieved by having your annual accounts checked and counter-signed by the association before your tax declaration. In effect, it is worth 20 per cent of your profit figure, as you will only be assessed on 80 per cent of your profit (if it is less than 701,000 FF) by the tax authorities if your accounts have been countersigned by an *association agréée*.

FINANCIAL CONSIDERATIONS FOR SELF-EMPLOYMENT

Making banking arrangements
You must have separate bank accounts for private and business accounts. If a bank is aware that one of your accounts is being used for business purposes, you may be required to pay higher bank charges. If necessary, to avoid these higher charges, open your business and personal accounts at different banks.

Accounting
You must keep correct accounts which conform to basic French accounting procedures. The easiest way to do this if you already have a computer is to buy an inexpensive personal computer program, which will correspond to the standard French tax form (number 2035).

Budgeting for your business
The table in Figure 8 (provided by an *association agréée*) gives you a good idea of how to budget for your activity. It has been prepared using contribution rates and figures valid for April 1998 and assuming a full twelve months of activity in each year. It is only intended as a very general guide to give you an idea of how and when and why you must plan for the cost of social charges in France.

For the first two years after establishing your business, you will be assessed for social charges on the basis of fixed contributions for health insurance, pensions and family allowance contributions. Your **CSG (contribution sociale generalisée)** and **RDS (recouvrement de la dette sociale)** payments are also included in the fixed contributions for the first two years of operating.

In the third year of operating, you will suddenly find that you face higher social charges and a significant CSG and RDS contribution. The figures in the column marked Year 3 in Figure 8 are the current April 1998 figures. The pension contribution currently stands at a

	YEAR 1	YEAR 2	YEAR 3	YEAR 4	YEAR 5	YEAR 6
Sales revenue	164000	236000	284000	350000	400000	200000
Operating expenses	50027	60832	76900	96050	112240	47360
Operating profit	113973	175168	207100	253950	287760	152640
Health	4000	4000	5400	8850	10620	12980
Pension (CIPAV)	4889	16084	16300	17000	17420	17980
Family allowances	5084	5084	5400	8100	9720	11880
Total social charges	13973	25168	27100	33950	37760	42840
CSG/RDS	included in family allowance payments for years 1 and 2		9118	14013	16568	20316
Net profit before tax	100000	150000	180000	220000	250000	109800
Profit assessed for income tax after 20% assoc. agréée reduction	80000	120000	144000	176000	200000	87840

Fig. 8. Budgeting for a non-salaried professional activity in France (source: AGIL).

total of 14,900 FF, plus 1.4 per cent of your net profit before tax from two years ago. The net profit before tax from two years ago is used to calculate health insurance (x 5.9%) and family allowance contributions (x 5.4%) from Year 3.

To budget for the sudden increase in CSG and RDS contributions, you should calculate 8 per cent of the sum of your net profit before tax two years ago, plus your total social charges for the same year.

Year 6 in Figure 8 has been deliberately designed to show the impact of a drop in sales revenue upon your budgeting. Since your contributions are based on your net profit from two years ago, you may find yourself heavily out of pocket if you do suffer a sudden downturn in business.

Working alone or in partnership

One consideration you may wish to make is whether to be truly **indépendant** or to work with a business partner (**associé**). This is a complex issue which requires professional advice, as certain investment and tax issues might favour a 'company' partnership of self-employed workers. Certain clients may also prefer the apparent security of dealing with a company rather than an individual. Amongst the options to explore are:

- Forming a company without any partners, **une Entreprise Unipersonnelle à Responsabilité Limitée** (or **EURL**). This is an alternative to being a **travailleur indépendant**. The minimum capital for an EURL is 50,000 FF.

- The 'means of business' – e.g. office premises or furniture, etc. – can be placed in common ownership, whilst each *professionel libéral* maintains his or her own clientele. There are several ways of achieving this, for which you should seek professional advice (e.g. from an *association agréée*).

- Associations in France, which are controlled by the law of 1901, can also be of use in making certain economies, as can **Groupement d'Intérêts Economique (GIE)**. It costs nothing to establish an *association 1901*, but in general they are designed to be non-profit-making. Any profit will be taxed on the basis of company tax rates. An *association 1901* is not allowed to distribute profits amongst its members. Once again, seek professional advice on this point.

None of these steps should be taken without professional advice. A good *association agréée* should be able to put you in contact with the appropriate professionals to discuss the best way forward.

'Multiple' employment

Pluriactivité, as it is known in France, has a number of important implications, which make it a generally unproductive option. This is principally because of the level of social charges involved:

1. **Several self-employed activities** – This will affect which **caisse d'assurance maladie** and which **caisse de vieillesse** you contribute to. If you are chosen to advise a public authority, you contribute to their funds. If you belong to a profession which has an 'order' (e.g. doctors or lawyers), you will contribute to their funds. In other cases, you have a fairly free choice according to the areas of activity in which you are engaged.

2. **A self-employed activity and a non-waged, 'non-libéral' activity** – You will be obliged to contribute to the same funds as above for the activity which brings you the highest revenue.

3. **Self-employment and paid employment** – You will be obliged to make payments to the **caisse de vieillesse** in both systems, even if your self-employment is a subsidiary activity. However, you will have rights under both systems. The same applies for the **caisse d'assurance maladie**. The difference is that only those services and rights offered by the *caisse* of your *principal* activity are available to you.

Professional restrictions

Certain professions – most notably lawyers and doctors – may not simply open up their own business in France without the agreement of the appropriate professional order. Contact your own professional association before moving to France to find out if you fall into one of these categories.

You should also note that certain professions – accountants, lawyers and doctors included – are not allowed to advertise their services under French advertising law. Any breach of this law can have very serious consequences. This may affect your ability to establish your own practice immediately upon arrival.

Making the final decision

If you are considering self-employment in France, you are probably already aware of the attractions of such a choice, most notably the entrepreneur's freedom of action.

However, listed below are a few of the factors you must consider before taking the plunge. Generally, it is better to seek salaried employment in France in order to establish yourself, rather than seeking to start a new business from nothing:

1. **Unemployment** – If your business fails, you have no right to unemployment benefits.

2. **Professional restrictions** – Are you allowed to practise in France, and how will you build up your clientele if you are not allowed to advertise?

3. **Heavy social charges** – On average, an employee costs a company in total double what he or she receives in their bank account each month. Being your own boss means paying the boss's share of the bill too. French social charges are amongst the highest in Europe.

    Worse still is the fact that after two years of operating, you are assessed on your profit figure from two years ago. If your sales suddenly drop, your difficulties will be increased by the fact that your social charges could rise to as much as 90 per cent of your current revenue, at the same time as your sales revenue falls (see Figure 8).

One final point – over 3,000 French companies now have 'head offices' (**siège sociale**) outside France in order to pay lower social charges. Many of these are based in the UK. Whilst this complies with European Union law, the French Ministry of Finance is seeking to fight back legally against the evasion of French social charges. As the French say, **à suivre...**

PAYING TAX IN FRANCE

Tax liability in France

You are liable for tax in France if you reside more than 183 days in France in any one calendar year. A double taxation agreement between France and the UK prevents those who still have tax liabilities in the UK from being taxed twice on the same element of income. This is the Convention for the Avoidance of Double Taxation and the

Prevention of Fiscal Evasion with respect to Taxes on Income.

Income tax (**impôt sur le revenu**) is payed in arrears. You will be required to complete a tax declaration, sent directly to your home, in March each year. This will be for the preceding tax year, which in France runs from 1 January to 31 December. If you send your declaration in late, you run the risk of a fine equivalent to a surcharge of an extra 10 per cent of your allotted tax bill.

If you do not reach your tax threshold by the end of the calendar year (e.g. you start work in September), you will be exempted from income tax for your first year in France. However, you must prepare yourself for your first tax bill when it does arrive, as you will be required to pay this in one lump sum. This is normally in about October or November, and is roughly equivalent to one month's salary. It is advisable to open a deposit account at the bank to prepare for this.

After the first lump sum payment, you will have the choice of paying monthly (**mensuelle**), or three times a year. You will also have the chance of paying by standing order, which the tax office will regulate, or by cheque.

It is important to bear in mind that you will therefore still have income tax to pay in France even if you leave France, for a limited period after your departure. As and when you do leave France, you should visit the tax office to 'sign off' their registers, and make the appropriate arrangements.

Tax bands in France

Income tax is progressive, ranging from 0 to 56.8 per cent. However, there are a variety of rebates and exemptions which are granted on gross income which moderate the rate of taxation. Most salaried workers receive not only the standard deduction of 10 per cent but also a further deduction of 20 per cent for the remaining figure.

Generally, families are favoured by the French tax system. 'Le Quotient Familial' means that taxable income is divided into units reflecting the family status of the family. Hence a single person is taxed on their whole income. A married couple are considered as two units, and their joint income will be divided by two. The first two children each count as a half-unit, and each additional child is counted as a full unit.

Wealth tax

Wealth Tax (**impôt sur la fortune**) for French residents is 0.5 per cent if your French assets are worth more than 4,390,000 FF. The rate then goes up progressively in bands. Assets worth in excess of 42,520,000 FF are subject to a tax of 1.5 per cent.

WORKING WITH CHILDREN

Traditionally this has been limited to young women in the 18–25-year-old age bracket, but young men of a similar age can and do find au pair work in France.

Au pairs and nannies
An au pair is generally a young person with no formal qualification in childcare, who lives as one of the family. She or he is paid a small sum of 'pocket money' (normally around 1,500–2,000 FF/month) in return for looking after the children, *light* housework and several evenings babysitting per week. Accommodation and meals are normally provided by the family. Au pairs normally take a language course during the daytime. This is obligatory for non-EU citizens as regards their residence permits.

Nannies have formal qualifications in childcare, and as such are much better paid. Their duties are much more restricted specifically to childcare, and accommodation is not normally provided. Both nannies and au pairs are often expected to travel with their families.

Looking for work
There are a number of agencies which place au pairs and nannies, both in the UK and in France (principally in Paris). It is quite possible to find a position before arriving in France, through such magazines as *The Lady*.

In Paris, the magazines *France-USA Contacts* and *The Free Voice* carry regular advertisements. You should also check noticeboards for small advertisements, and place advertisements seeking work in the same places. There are generally more jobs available than au pairs to fill them, so you should not feel stuck if your first family does not prove satisfactory.

Conditions of employment
Au pairing falls within one of the 'grey' areas of French employment. There are set guidelines, but making sure that these are applied is not always easy. Establishing a good relation not only with the children but also with 'Monsieur et Madame' is vital to a successful stay.

Generally, you will be employed from September to June, although you may well be asked to stay and help in the summer holiday months. Your employer *should* make a **déclaration d'engagement** to the social security office. In reality, few employers will do this voluntarily as they fear paying extra taxes to pay for your statutory rights. If you are an EU citizen, make sure you take the E111 form with you to France to cover emergency health care.

Accommodation and travel

If you are lucky, you will have accommodation in the separate **chambre de bonne** – cold and damp in winter, perhaps with a shared toilet, but an oasis of privacy from the children! In Paris, it is customary to pay half the *carte orange* travel pass for all employees. Travel may be to the family home deep in the country, where you will find yourself perhaps looking after more children than you bargained on. But the upside is that you could also be taken skiing, for instance.

Documents

Non-EU nationals will require a long-term stay visa, which means that you must have the **déclaration d'engagement** and a registration certificate at a language school. EU nationals should remember that they cannot stay in France legally more than three months without a *carte de séjour*, and so they too do need a *déclaration*.

CASUAL AND SEASONAL WORK

Seasonal work is less easy to find in the current difficult economic climate. Work is more likely to be found in the larger cities than in rural or resort areas. You must accept that by its very nature, the kind of work you will probably find will probably be poorly paid and unexciting. If you have good office skills, you may find work more easily via the agencies which supply temporary staff. The larger department stores often recruit extra staff in sales periods.

UNEMPLOYMENT IN FRANCE

Unemployment is dealt with by two agencies in France. The ANPE is the local job centre, where you must be registered if you are out of work and seeking to claim unemployment benefit. The ASSEDIC is the agency which actually pays you unemployment benefit, if you qualify.

Jobseekers from other EU countries

You have the right to seek work in France for three months before you will have officially 'outstayed your welcome'. During that three-month period, if you are registered as unemployed in your home country, you will retain your right to receive unemployment benefits from your home country via the French unemployment benefit service, the ASSEDIC.

In order to obtain these benefits, you need to complete and bring with you two EU social security forms:

- **The E303** – You must present this at your local **ANPE (Agence Nationale pour l'Emploi** – the job centre) **within seven days of your arrival**. You must also register at the ANPE at the same time.

- **The E119** – This will provide you with full medical cover for the three-month period during which you are entitled to stay in France and seek work. To establish your health rights during this period, contact your local **CPAM (Caisse Primaire d'Assurance Maladie** – the local health authority), and ask for details of how to contact the nearest **Service des Relations International**.

Unemployment rights for French residents

If you are employed in France and are unfortunate enough to lose your job, you will start to appreciate the heavy social charges that you paid when you were in employment.

Qualifying for unemployment benefit
- If you resign without good reason, are dismissed for a **faute grave** (serious misconduct) or refuse a suitable job offer, you will be refused unemployment benefit on the grounds that you do not wish to work.

- To qualify, you must have worked at least three months in the last year, and for two of the three last years. You must also be under 60.

- You must register at the local ANPE, and be both capable of work and actively seeking employment.

The **allocation d'assurance chômage** (unemployment benefit) you receive depends on how much you have paid into the system and over what period of time, i.e. if you have been working for four years on an average wage, you will receive more than if you have been working on the minimum wage for the last two years. Payments may take some time to come through initially, but are backdated.

The amount of your *allocation* will diminish with time, as you effectively use up the fund you have created during the time you were employed by yours and your former employer's contributions. After two years, your situation will be reassessed and you will receive a reduced *allocation*. The next stage after that, known as the RMI, is the very basic minimum aid which is given out. Once that has been exhausted, you are not entitled to any further benefit.

You must be careful to keep copies of job searches and applications during the time that you are *en chômage*. This will be required by the ASSEDIC and the ANPE to justify your continued benefit payments.

Help for the unemployed

Your social security rights, if they are already established, will remain intact throughout the time that you continue to receive unemployment benefits. Even after you have used up the right to the RMI, you will have social security rights under the French system for one further year.

The **Service Sociale** at your local mairie also has a fund at its disposal to help in cases of difficulty and emergency, e.g. the electricity is about to be cut off. The amount of aid available depends entirely on your local mairie, and may only be a token contribution towards clearing your debts.

Redundancy due to economic cut-backs

If you are made redundant due to cut-backs in the firm, you will have 'first refusal' for your job should it be re-created subsequently. In terms of your financial situation, you can also request a *convention conversion* which will allow you to draw 80 per cent of your final salary for a limited period (normally six months).

CHECKLIST

1. Have you made sufficient financial planning to support yourself through the initial stages of job searching in France?

2. Have you gathered together all the appropriate paperwork, such as jobseekers' entitlement forms?

3. How much can your prepare in advance for job applications in France? Get hold of copies of French newspapers with job advertisements, prepare a French CV and practise writing French application letters.

6
Retiring in France

If you decide to spend your twilight years in a place in the sun in France, there are a great many preparations to be made. It is difficult to establish 'hard and fast' rules, as everybody's personal circumstances are so different.

Nevertheless, the basic administrative steps that must be taken – securing a residence permit and enrolling in the French social security system, not to mention making arrangements for pension payments – all require careful attention. Do not be fooled by the notion of 'free movement' of workers and citizens within the European Union (EU). Moving is not a problem; staying can be, if it is not handled properly.

There are also important considerations to make when purchasing property in France. The basic outlines given in Chapter 4 are still the same. However, you must plan carefully for the future when purchasing. The system of purchasing that you choose will have very serious consequences when questions of succession and ownership arise after death.

THE PENSION SCHEME IN FRANCE

If you are already working in France and paying into the French social security system, retirement age in France is 60 for both men and women. This is when they become eligible for their state and supplementary pensions to which they have contributed during their working lives.

Your insurance record takes into account periods of absence from work (including sickness, work accidents, maternity leave or unemployment). Pensions are then calculated on the following basic formula:

$$\frac{\text{basic wage x period insured}}{160}$$

To receive a full pension, you must now have contributed for at least

40 years (as opposed to 37.5 years previously). The maximum state pension possible is equal to 50 per cent of your average earnings in your 10 highest paid years. A reduced pension is equivalent to $\frac{1}{160}$ of the full pension x number of quarters' insurance you have paid.

State pensions are indexed to take account of rises in the cost of living. Supplementary pensions depend on the number of points you have accumulated during your working life up to the age of 60. Added together with the state pension, the complementary pension normally brings a retirement pension income up to about 80 per cent of your final salary at retirement, for those who have contributed continuously to both schemes.

You need to apply for your pension entitlements about three to four months before the date you plan to retire. For this you will need to complete a **demande de retraite personelle**. Contact your local health authority (**caisse primaire d'assurance maladie**) for further details.

OBTAINING A RESIDENCE PERMIT

As with any EU citizen moving to live in France, you must obtain a **carte de séjour** within three months of your arrival. Details of how to do this are explained in Chapter 3. However, if you are intending to retire to France, you will be asked to produce additional documentation:

- A **Justificatif des Ressources** — normally this will be a bank reference which has been translated by an approved translator. You will certainly need proof of all the money at your disposal (including pension entitlements). Enquire at the nearest French consulate *before* coming to France in order to establish what precisely will be required.

- You may also be required to produce a medical certificate. Once again, check this with your local consulate before coming to France, or the préfecture when you arrive. It only seems to be demanded in certain random cases – but be prepared. Evidence of medical insurance may also be required.

The residence permit you will receive as a retired person will quite specifically state that you are *not* allowed to undertake paid employment or self-employment. If you wish to undertake any form of consultancy work, for instance, you must enquire at your local préfecture for the correct procedure and paperwork required for your residence permit.

TRANSFERRING HEALTH AND WELFARE RIGHTS

EU citizens are covered by reciprocal arrangements within the EU allowing them to transfer their rights to another member country. Chapters 4 and 7 also contain information relating to handicap and disability which may be of interest either now or in the future.

Reaching retirement age

If you have already reached retirement age (60), or will have reached retirement age when you move abroad, you need to obtain **Form E121**. To apply for this form in the UK, write to The Contributions Agency, International Services, Department of Social Security, Longbenton, Newcastle upon Tyne NE98 1YX. The International Services Helpline is 0645 154811; Fax: 0645 157800. From France, Tel: 00 44 191 225 4811; or Fax: 00 44 191 225 7800.

You should make arrangements to obtain Form E121 as early as possible before you leave for France. The E121 is valid indefinitely. When you arrive in France, take it along to your local *caisse primaire d'assurance maladie*. As the same time you must take either your *carte de séjour*, or the receipt (**récipissé**). You will then be enrolled under the French social security system.

Taking early retirement

If you are taking early retirement, you will need to enquire at the Contributions Agency about **Form E106**. This will grant healthcare cover for a limited period, after which you will need to make voluntary contributions to the French system.

Taking out private health insurance

It is highly advisable to be a member of a private health insurance scheme even if you make all the appropriate arrangements for transferring your rights under the state systems. If you transfer your rights into the French system, and subsequently return to the UK and/or fall ill whilst there, no private scheme in the UK will admit or readmit you over the age of 65. You will thus be left with minimal coverage at just the time of life when you are most likely to need it – or the prospect of a very heavy bill for private care.

You should also bear in mind that you will not be eligible for any assistance from the UK government if eventually you need to be admitted to a private nursing home or residential home in France.

CLAIMING YOUR PENSION

Claiming a UK retirement pension abroad

If you are entitled to a UK state pension, you can ask for a retirement pension forecast from the Contributions Agency (see above). The pension forecast will tell you the current level of your pension, and whether or not there are any ways of improving that level. You will not need to do this if you are within four months of retirement, as you will be contacted automatically by the DSS.

You can receive a UK retirement pension, and also war pensions and widows' benefits, in any EU country. The amount you receive will be the same as in the UK, although you must take into account exchange rates. You will also benefit from annual increases in the pension rate if you live within the EU.

You can choose to have the money paid to you:

● directly into your bank account abroad

● *or* into a UK bank or building society

● *or* into the account of a pension of your choice

● *or* sent to your address abroad, either every 4 or every 13 weeks, or annually for small sums.

Claiming pensions from more than one EU country

If you have been employed in more than one EU country – for instance, France and the UK – you will have paid insurance into both systems. As long as you meet the rules of both countries, you will be entitled to a pension from each system.

Each country will work out the pension due to you under their own national system. They will also look at the amount of pension due to you from the other country concerned. This can help you to get a pension, or even a higher pension, under their own national system. They do this by working out how much pension you would be entitled to if all your contributions had been paid into one national system.

Whilst the paperwork is flying back and forth, you will be paid your pension from each system, according simply to what you have paid into that system. However, if it is discovered that the totality of your contributions entitles you to a higher pension, you will eventually receive this without having to ask.

Paying tax on your pension

Pensions are taxable in France, but on a much lower scale than for those in active employment or self-employment. If you are moving to France from the UK, contact your local tax office in the UK to make arrangements for qualifying as a non-resident, and therefore being exempted from British tax duties. In France, you must then contact your local **centre des impôts** to register for French income tax.

BUYING YOUR RETIREMENT HOME

Chapter 4 gives you a basic outline of the process which is involved in purchasing property in France. You should also refer to *How to Rent & Buy Property in France* by Clive Kristen.

Choosing where to buy

When you are choosing where to buy your retirement home in France, you need to consider a number of factors, especially if you are looking at property in rural areas:

● What transport links are near to the property? You may *think* you want to be a million miles from anywhere and anyone. In reality, if something goes wrong, you do not want to be too far from the emergency and medical services, not to mention essential shops. Also, what will happen when you are no longer able to drive your own car?

● If your idea of hell is other people, you may discover that hell is in fact not having other people around. Certain parts of France are very sparsely populated indeed, and there is a continuing concern over rural 'desertification'. Whilst this means that you may well be welcomed to an area because you are intending to renovate a derelict property, it may also mean neighbours are very few and far between.

   French provincial social life revolves mainly around the entertainment of a person's own family. Even if you have a lot of visitors (as is often the case), this may not really compensate for the lack of society to which you are accustomed. Regional associations (see the Regional Directory) may be able to help fill this gap; but not all regions offer the same possibilities.

● Buying a property in France, especially in a rural area, is normally a lot easier than trying to sell it again afterwards. French buyers are normally on the look out for properties that can be easily renovated to make holiday homes. The type of property which you may well purchase probably will not fall into this category. Also, there is the problem of a potential buyer securing a mortgage.

Obviously certain areas of France and their property markets are more popular than others. What you may have to remember is that if you bought a house for a 'bargain' price, you may well have to sell it at a similar rate if you ever want to be free of it in years to come.

Looking at inheritance issues

It is extremely important that you take good professional advice when buying your property in France, as regards questions of ownership and inheritance. You must do this before you sign the contracts; afterwards, it will be too late. You should also bear in mind that the legal system is both very slow and very expensive in France.

The main thing to watch out for is that the notaire does not draw up a contract whereby you buy the property **en division**. The much more preferable option is to buy **en tontine**. There are other possibilities (e.g. an **acte de donation**); but you will need to discuss these with your legal advisers.

Problems with buying a property *en division*

If you and your spouse buy a property *en division*, you will each own half of the property. When one of you dies, the 'half' which belongs to the deceased person will pass automatically to his/her heirs. The situation then is that the surviving spouse may then own half a house, with a right of abode for the remainder of their life.

If you have children, you cannot leave your half of your property to your spouse. You can leave part of it to your spouse, but he/she will be liable for Succession Tax on the part they have inherited. If there are more than three children, they automatically inherit three-quarters of the deceased person's estate. Succession Tax is then payable immediately, even if the surviving spouse continues living in the house.

The house cannot be sold to pay the Succession Tax without the consent of the surviving spouse, nor if one of the children is under eighteen years old.

DEALING WITH BEREAVEMENT

After dealing with the Here, you need also to be prepared for the Hereafter. According to the American poet Emily Dickinson, 'Parting is all we know of heaven, And all we need of hell.' Like most other things in France, dying is not as easy as one might imagine it to be! For those left behind 'hell' can also refer to the necessary paperwork.

Quite apart from the personal emotional situation which has to be dealt with, there are numerous administrative tasks to be undertaken. These concern not only winding up a deceased person's estate, but also putting your own affairs in order.

Immediately after the death

1. The death certificate (**certificat de constatation de décès**) must be signed and certified by a doctor.

2. Within 24 hours of death, the death must be registered (**déclaration de décès**) at the mairie of the place where the death occurred. For this, you need proof of identity, the death certificate, and proof of identity (*carte de séjour*, birth or marriage certificate) of the deceased.

3. After registering the death, you will be given the **acte de décès** which is the official death certificate required by banks and administrative offices, etc. You can ask for several copies of the certificate straight away to avoid delays in dealing with the next round of paperwork.

Arranging the funeral

The undertaker (**pompes funèbres**) can arrange all the certificates as part of the services offered. Before you go ahead with the funeral service, you will need a burial permit (**permis d'inhumer**). The earliest that this can take place is 24 hours after the death, and at the latest six days after the death. Burial is still by far the most common form of funeral in France, and crematoria are relatively rare. Nor are they as 'user-friendly' as in the UK or the USA.

The burial must take place in the local cemetery of the village or commune where the deceased lived, unless s/he had purchased a burial plot (**concession**) in another cemetery. If you wish to arrange a burial in another commune or village, you will require the authorisation of the local mairie.

The cost of a burial is currently in the region of 20,000–30,000FF. In addition to this, you will also be faced with a bill for the purchase of a burial plot and tombstone. If you want the burial to take place in your home country, you will need to make enquiries as to the likely costs involved for transportation. Although financial assets are officially frozen initially (see below), most banks or financial institutions will release about 20,000 FF to the immediate family for funeral expenses.

Informing creditors and debtors

The following people must all be notified of a death within a week:

- All banks, savings plans, etc. where the deceased had an account. Joint accounts will need to be converted into personal accounts.

- Any credit organisations where loans had been taken out.

- All insurance companies, and especially life insurance companies.

- The local health authority (**CPAM**), the local pensions unit (**caisse vieillesse**), and any other welfare units who were issuing benefits to the deceased. If the deceased received a complementary French pension, then that *caisse* must also be informed.

- The landlord if the deceased was renting property. If the deceased was renting his/her property to somebody else, then the tenants must be informed to whom they should now pay their rent.

- If the deceased lived in an apartment in a *copropriété*, the Syndic must be informed also.

Wills and inheritance

Normally you will need to use the services of a **notaire** (equivalent to a solicitor), only if there is any dispute over the will amongst the legatees, or if the deceased was the owner of property. If the deceased was not a property owner, and left only furniture, bank accounts, etc., then as long as there is no dispute amongst the legatees, there is no need to involve a notaire.

If the deceased owned property, you must use the services of a notaire to take the necessary steps. The principal role of the notaire if s/he is involved will be to issue the **attestation de propriété des biens immobiliers**, which will permit the legatees to inherit the property legally. Rather like the undertaker, s/he can also undertake other administrative tasks for you which can make life easier at a difficult time. These include dealing with social security offices, the tax offices and tenants. His/her other functions are:

- checking on any unknown claimants on the deceased's estate

- checking the terms of a will or an *acte de donation* between a married couple

- checking that each legatee has received the correct portion left to him/her under the terms of the will and French law.

Tax issues

Tax issues are one area where you may well be pleased to benefit from the expertise of a notaire, if you are not happy dealing with the tax office yourself. A **déclaration de succession** is normally only necessary if the amount concerned is in excess of 100,000 FF. If the sum is less than 100,000 FF, and the inheritance is in 'direct succession' (spouse to spouse, parent to child), then the declaration to the tax office is not obligatory.

One declaration can be made on behalf of all the legatees, and must be made within six months of the death at the tax office of the deceased. Normally any payment due must be made at the same time as the declaration.

Tax declarations will have to be made in the name of the deceased (within six months of the death). For the surviving spouse, the tax declaration will have to be made at the usual time in the year (March), taking into account revenue acquired between the date of death and the end of the year. The surviving spouse and any children still benefit from the same number of 'parts' as if the deceased were still alive. For further clarification, speak to your local tax office in France.

COPING ON YOUR OWN

Health and welfare rights for widows and their children

If you had French health and social security rights on account of your late spouse's rights, you and your children will retain these rights, under the following conditions:

1.   For one year from the date of death, or until your last child reaches the age of three.

2.   If you have at least three children, you will then still keep your rights.

3.   If you receive single parent payments, or benefit from a **pension de réversion** or the **assurance veuvage** (see below), your health expenses will automatically be reimbursed.

If you do not fall into any of the categories above, then you must make a personal application to the Sécurité Sociale to be registered.

Claiming UK widows' benefits

You can continue to receive widows' benefit when you move abroad.

Arrangements for transferring this benefit are similar to those for transferring pension payments. Once again, you will receive annual increases to the benefit. To arrange for payment, you must contact The Benefits Agency, Pensions & Overseas Benefits Directorate, Department of Social Security, Tyneview Park, Whitley Road, Benton, Newcastle upon Tyne NE98 1BA. (Tel: (0191) 21 87777).

You may be able to claim this benefit if your husband dies whilst you were both living abroad if your husband had the necessary National Insurance record in the UK, or if you return to the UK within four weeks of his death.

All the above rules also apply for the payment of widowed mothers' allowance from the UK social security system. However, you cannot claim both benefits – only one or the other.

Claiming French widows' benefits

If you are widowed in France, and your late spouse was contributing to the French social security system as an active worker, you will be entitled to a number of financial aids:

* **Le capital-décès** – a lump-sum payment based on social security contributions and the employment record up till the time of death of your spouse. It is designed to act as an emergency measure to cover immediate difficulties due to a loss of salary from the deceased. The deceased must not have ceased active employment for more than 12 months at the time the death occurred. Normally the amount is about three times the last monthly salary of the deceased. Applications for this sum should be made at the local *caisse primaire d'assurance maladie* of the deceased.

* **L'allocation de parent isolé** – a limited period minimum revenue payment for single parents. The amount paid is the difference between your own resources and the minimum amount guaranteed under this benefit.

* **L'assurance veuvage** – this is assistance for widows under the age of 55 who are raising children. As with the *pension de réversion* (below), it is means-tested.

* **La pension de réversion du régime de retraite de base** – this is a means-tested way of deciding if you are entitled to continue claiming a reduced basic state pension earnt by your late spouse. It is currently equivalent to 54 per cent of the last pension paid to

the deceased. You must be at least 55 years old to be considered for this benefit.

If you do not qualify on the first application, you can re-apply. If you are awarded this pension, and even if you remarry, you will continue to receive this pension for the rest of your life. This also applies even if your financial situation improves also. To apply for this pension, contact the *caisse de retraite* of your late spouse.

- **La pension de réversion du régime de retraite complémentaire** – this is not means-tested. Generally speaking, the surviving spouse is entitled to receive 60 per cent of the complementary pension that the deceased received, or would have received if s/he was still working at the time of their death. Contact the *caisse d'assurance vieillesse* concerned to apply for this pension.

CHECKLIST

1. Make sure you have up-to-date bank statements and other proofs of your financial resources ready for your residence permit application. See the checklist in Chapter 3 to make sure that you have all the necessary documents for this application.

2. Contact the appropriate social security agencies to arrange for the transfer of pensions and benefits. Make sure that you have applied for Form E121 (and E106 if appropriate) in good time.

3. Check out private healthcare options available to you. Which companies/packages offer the best possibilities for you?

4. Contact your local tax office to arrange to be declared non-resident. You must then contact your new local tax office in France in order to register.

5. Seek legal advisers who can help you with property contracts, wills and tax issues. Money well spent will be a wise investment for the future.

6. Consider carefully the 'pros' and 'cons' of a particular property and its location before signing anything. Do not let your heart rule your head, and be practical about the future.

7
Looking at Health and Welfare

For British citizens, it is essential that you obtain copies of the Department of Social Security pamphlets **Social Security Abroad** Number NI38 and **Your social security insurance, benefits and health care rights in the European Community** Number SA29. Both of these comprehensive pamphlets are free from: Department of Social Security, Overseas Branch, Newcastle upon Tyne NE98 1YX. Separate leaflets are available from the Northern Ireland Social Security Agency International Services at 24–42, Corporation Street, Belfast BT1 3DP.

There used to be a joke amongst British expatriates that the standard remedy for any medical problem in France was to prescribe suppositories. This is not only untrue, but distracts from the reality that French healthcare is generally of a very high standard. Critics might retaliate, however, that this is because the French are a nation of hypochondriacs, which at times it is hard to dispute.

The cost of sometimes over-generous healthcare has certainly been a bitter pill to swallow in recent years. French doctors will not generally prescribe just one drug to cure a complaint, but several. Attempts to limit stockpiling of half-used medicines have provoked outrage, but are gradually being pursued as the French come to terms with their huge social security bill.

JOINING THE SOCIAL SECURITY SYSTEM

If you are living and working in France, you are obliged to join the French **Sécurité Sociale,** covering pensions, sickness and healthcare, and unemployment. Generally, you will need certified copies of your birth and marriage certificates as for your carte de séjour. Check with your employer and/or your local social security office.

- If you are in regular employment in France, this will happen almost automatically courtesy of your employer. Both you and your employer must make regular contributions to ensure that you and your dependants are adequately covered.

● If you are self-employed, you pay a percentage of your taxable income as your contribution which will then be deductible for income tax purposes. Self-employed workers are not covered in the same way as employed workers by the Sécurité Sociale. It is therefore important that you join the appropriate scheme as soon as possible after arriving in France. For further details, see Chapter 5 on Working in France.

● If you are a UK national sent to work in France for less than twelve months, you will normally remain insured under the UK National Insurance scheme. You or your employer should obtain the appropriate forms (E101 and E111) from the DSS Overseas Branch, Newcastle upon Tyne NE98 IYX, before coming to France. These prove that you remain insured under the British system, and entitle you to emergency medical care. (See also below.)

● If you are retiring to France, see Chapter 6.

● If you are unemployed and come to France to look for work, or you are working as an au pair, see Chapter 5 on Working in France.

● If you are studying in France, see Chapter 8. If you are an EU citizen, you will need to obtain the form E111.

The Sécurité Sociale is notoriously slow in issuing numbers, cards and reimbursement. You may have to wait some time until you receive your card demonstrating your eligibility to use state services, and for reimbursement. Medical treatment will only be reimbursed after proof that you have worked 200 hours in the previous three months. This can include time worked in the UK. Form E104 available from the DSS in Newcastle upon Tyne will need to be completed and submitted by your French employer.

If you are in paid employment in France, and are therefore enrolled in the French Social Security system, your spouse, partner (if they are totally dependent on you financially), your children under 16 years of age, or up to 20 years of age if they are studying, are all covered by your social security payments for standard medical treatment and reimbursement.

WORKING ABROAD FOR A FIXED PERIOD

Medical records
If you inform the DSS Contributions Department that you are going to live or work abroad for a limited period (e.g. because you or your partner have been seconded), they will automatically inform the National Health Service Central Register. They will amend the Central Index of Patients which helps to determine funding for each Family Health Service Authority (FHSA).

The FHSA will in turn withdraw your medical records from your general practitioner about nine months after your departure. Your records will either be held until you return or re-register with a new doctor, or until they are destroyed. Records are normally held for at least six years.

If you are going abroad for a limited period and plan to return to your current home area, it may be useful to inform your general practitioner of both your departure and your anticipated return date. This will avoid your records being withdrawn unnecessarily.

Maintaining your social security rights
The DSS pamphlet NI38 explains in detail how to go about maintaining your British social security rights (if you have them) whilst working abroad. It is very important that you read this pamphlet and take advice based on the information which it provides. This can affect your eligibility for state benefits upon your return to the UK, and your pension rights later in life.

Voluntary contributions can also be made in some circumstances, but these will not automatically entitle you to French social security benefits. They will simply guarantee your right to apply for British benefits.

IMMUNISATION

Standard immunisations are always worthwhile, although there are no particular dangers associated with life in France. Frequent contact with former French colonies in Africa may possibly mean that certain diseases are more common in France than in the UK or the USA, but the extra risks are minimal. All vaccines are available on prescription in France from chemist's shops, and can be administered by qualified doctors.

GENERAL PRACTITIONERS

In France you are not limited to registering with one general practitioner in your area. You are free to consult as many doctors as you wish, as often as you wish, wherever you wish. The French frequently take advantage of this system to ask for second or even third opinions, but it is not really advisable unless you doubt the competence or approach of your doctor.

Sticking to one doctor allows him or her to know you and your problems better. The government is now actively encouraging doctors and patients to build 'exclusive' relationships, to cut back on the amount of money spent reimbursing multiple doctors' appointment fees.

Each time you visit the doctor, you will be asked to pay a consultation fee (**honoraire**) currently of either 115 FF or 140 FF – the price depends on the system the doctor works within (see below). Make sure that the doctor completes and signs a brown **feuille de soin** which you will need to reclaim this cost. The level at which you will be reimbursed for standard doctors' fees is currently about 65 per cent.

GOING TO THE CHEMIST'S

At the chemist's shop (**pharmacie**), indicated by a green cross, hand over the prescription (**ordonnance**) and the **feuille de soin** to the pharmacist. Once your medicines have been prepared, you will be asked to pay in full. The pharmacist should enter the cost of the drugs on the reverse side of the **feuille de soin,** and also stick on the small labels (**vignettes**) from the medicine boxes. Without these labels, the cost of the drugs will not be reimbursed.

The level of reimbursement for medicines varies from nothing up to 100 per cent if you have obtained an exemption certificate proving that the drug(s) are essential to your well-being. Chemist's shops provide a rota of weekend cover, which is posted clearly in shop windows along with details of late-opening chemists.

Finding the medicines that you need

Most medicines are available in France, but may be marketed under a different name. It is very worthwhile checking this with your regular pharmacy, or even the drug company, before moving to France. Another good idea is to take the packaging listing the ingredients with you, so that the doctor can check the components against a similar product in the 'Bible' he or she always consults before prescribing.

Over-the-counter drugs are available in more or less the same way as in the UK. Chemists will advise you as to cost and value of the products you require. Paracetamol and aspirin are both known under the same names.

Obtaining exemption certificates

If you have a disability or disease which requires regular and/or expensive medication, you may be eligible for an exemption certificate (**pris en charge**). Normally this will cover 100 per cent of all fees associated with treatment, including medicines.

You will need to speak to your general practitioner or hospital specialist to arrange this. It is not an easy process, and can take a long time. The availability of such help can also vary from area to area, according to the local health authority budget. You will certainly need thorough medical documentation and a recommendation from a French doctor, and will be summoned to 'demonstrate' your disability or disease by a local health authority doctor (**medecin conseil**). Exemptions are also sometimes granted for a limited period after an accident and during the convalescence period.

REIMBURSEMENT

Once you have a complete **feuille de soin,** fill in the personal details, including social security number and means of payment (direct debit or cheque), and send it to your local social security centre (**caisse primaire d'assurance maladie – CPAM**) where your file (**dossier**) is held. Keep a copy of each **feuille de soin** sent.

After several weeks, you will eventually be reimbursed if all the paperwork is in order, and will receive a statement of how much you have been reimbursed for each expense. A new scheme, first tested in April 1998, will eventually replace both the social security card and the **feuille de soin** with a personalised health credit card (**carte au puce**), simplifying and speeding up the reimbursement procedure.

The DSS Form E111 available from British post offices will provide British citizens with emergency healthcare cover for up to three months from the date of issue. However, the level of cover is limited to emergencies. Reimbursement can take place in either France or the UK. Private health insurance will provide a fuller cover for a visit of several months.

COMPLEMENTARY HEALTH INSURANCE

The remaining part of your expenditure on treatment or medicines can be reimbursed by joining a **mutuelle,** which is the standard French private health scheme. If you are in paid employment, you will almost always find that you are automatically included in such a scheme. Contributions are deducted each month along with regular social security contributions, and will be indicated on your pay-slip.

Almost every trade and profession has its own **mutuelle,** and it is very worthwhile belonging to such a scheme. Benefits can also include extra sick pay, a 'top up' to retirement pensions, and the ability to use private clinics if necessary or if you prefer.

LOOKING AT HOSPITAL TREATMENT

Every large town has at least one **hôpital conventionné** which acts as the local general hospital, and includes the casualty unit (**urgences**). You have a free choice as to whether to enter a public hospital (providing you do not arrive in emergency!) or a private clinic. However, there are certain differences as regards reimbursement for the cost of your healthcare.

Private hospital treatment will only be reimbursed by the **Sécurité Sociale** at the same rate as treatment in a **hôpital conventionné.** If you chose a private clinic, you will be given a form which must be validated by your local health authority centre, where your file is held. Once this has been validated, you hand this back to the clinic at your admission.

Your local *caisse d'assurance maladie* will settle the largest part of your hospital bill (80 per cent) if you are in a public hospital. Remember that private clinics will charge more for their services, and that you will only be reimbursed on the basis of a stay in a public hospital. The outstanding 20 per cent (or more for private treatment) is at your cost. Hospital treatment is thus the moment that you will most appreciate financially the benefits of a **mutuelle.**

In all cases you will be asked to pay the **forfait journalier** (currently 70 FF), which is basically a 'board and lodging' fee. You will normally also be offered the chance to hire your own telephone, and sometimes also a TV. Rooms are normally shared, except for those cases which require isolation.

There are numerous situations where your entire medical bill (i.e. not just the usual 80 per cent), except the *forfait journalier*, will be paid entirely for you by your local *caisse*. For example:

- important surgery

- if you are in hospital more than 31 days

- delivery of a baby (for a stay of up to 12 days) – nor in this case are you obliged to pay the *forfait journalier*

- if your admission is due to a work accident – once again, the *forfait journalier* is not charged

- if you are receiving invalidity payments or benefit due to a work accident

- if you are suffering from a serious illness which requires expensive medical care (as recognised by your local *caisse*).

You may also find that certain minor operations and clinical tests will take place during the course of one day, in which case you will be assigned a bed and admitted only for the day (**hôpital du jour**).

DENTAL CARE AND EYE CARE

The same rules apply for visits to the **dentiste** or the **opthalmologist** (optician) as apply to visiting a general practitioner. The optician will simply provide the prescription for your glasses or contact lenses, and you must then go to one of the many specialist shops in order to choose your frames or lenses.

POINTS TO REMEMBER:

1. It is very important to check if the medical practitioners and services you use – doctor, dentist, optician, hospital, physiotherapist, etc. – are **conventionné**. There is nothing to stop you using private medicine, but you must be able to bear the cost.

2. About 20 per cent of doctors are **non-conventionné**. Their fees are reimbursed much less by the **Sécurité Sociale and mutuelles.** Practitioners who are **coventionné à honoraires libres** charge variable prices. The **Sécurité Sociale** will reimburse at their fixed rate, and the **mutuelle** normally covers the rest of the cost.

3. Make sure that all practitioners complete a **feuille de soin** and return this to you after each consultation. Also make sure that pharmacists similarly complete their part of the *feuille*, and attach the **vignettes** from the medicine boxes.

HEALTH IN THE WORKPLACE

The French commitment to healthcare includes the firm doctor (**médecin de travail**). You will be expected to undergo a medical examination by this doctor, and paid for by the firm:

- when you join the company
- regularly once a year thereafter
- after a prolonged absence due to illness
- after pregnancy leave.

You also have the right to ask to see this doctor on request, and you may also be obliged to see the doctor at the request of your company. These doctors also carry out 'spot-checks' on your working conditions.

SICK LEAVE AND SICK PAY

Under French law, absence due to illness during the first year of your contract is not paid leave. Application of this law is, however, often at the discretion of the firm.

If you are obliged to take time off work due to illness, ask the doctor for a sick note (**arrêt de travail**). You should complete and sign this paper, and send one copy to your employer, one copy to the Sécurité Sociale, and keep one copy for yourself. The note will specify the length of absence permitted, and will also designate the hours in which you may go out to buy provisions, etc. **You must send off this note to your employer and your** *caisse* **within 48 hours.**

Be warned – the Sécurité Sociale regularly undertake random investigations to see if you are obeying the terms of the note. If you are not there when the inspector calls, the Sécurité Sociale can and will refuse to reimburse the firm for part of your salary during your absence. You could also face disciplinary proceedings.

Your employer will continue to pay you during your absence, but will recover part of the cost from your *caisse d'assurance maladie*. Your entitlement depends on having completed a certain number of hours of work. If your inability to work lasts less than six months, your eligibility will depend upon your having worked 200 hours in the last three months. If your inability is more serious and requires a longer period off work, eligibility for sick pay requires you to have worked at least twelve months, with at least 200 hours work in the last three months.

Sick pay is subject to income tax, and basically you will receive half your normal daily pay. Maternity pay or monies paid as a result of a work accident are not subject to income tax.

FAMILY MATTERS

Pregnancy healthcare

If you are a British citizen and pregnant at the time of moving to France, you should speak to your doctor and local health authority to find out what steps you need to take to ensure your health and benefit entitlements. You may need to obtain the form E112. To apply for this, write to: The Department of Health International Relations, Room 512, Richmond House, 79 Whitehall, London SW1A 2NS.

You must declare your pregnancy before the end of the third month to your **caisse d'assurance maladie,** and to the **caisse d'allocations familiales** (family benefit centre). To do this you must hand in the '**premier examen médical parental'** form duly signed by your doctor. You will receive a '**carnet de maternité'** which contains vouchers allowing you to receive the services to which you are entitled.

The services to which you are entitled free of charge are:

- pre-natal and post-natal examinations
- 8 pre-natal sessions to help you prepare for the delivery
- 12 days of free hospital treatment in a **conventionné** hospital or clinic or one which is '**agréé** (approved)
- from the first day of the sixth month of pregnancy, all medical expenses, whether related to the pregnancy or not, reimbursed by the *caisse* at 100 per cent (except certain types of drugs).

These rights are limited by the number of hours worked and the amount of money you have paid – or your husband or partner has paid – over the preceding months.

Maternity leave pay

Once again, the number of hours and level of contributions made is one of the deciding factors in whether you receive paid maternity leave. You must also have been enrolled in the Sécurité Sociale at least ten months by the expected date of delivery of your baby.

To obtain maternity pay, you must send the **attestation** (form) signed by your employer to the *caisse d'assurance maladie* as soon as you begin your maternity leave. You must then send a similar form to the *caisse* at the end of your maternity leave. The pay is calculated on the basis of your salary for three months before you stopped work, and works out at 84 per cent of your daily wage.

If you are already receiving Maternity Allowance when you leave the UK, you may be able to persuade your British social security office to carry on providing that benefit.

Maternity leave
For a first or second child, the normal leave period is six weeks before delivery and ten weeks afterwards. From the third child onwards, it is eight weeks before delivery and eighteen weeks afterwards. For twins, it is 12 weeks before delivery and 22 weeks afterwards; and for triplets (or more!) it is 24 weeks before delivery and 22 weeks afterwards. In the case of premature delivery, the total leave period is not reduced. In cases of medical necessity, a doctor may prescribe an extra two weeks.

Registering the birth
You **MUST** register the birth of your new child *within three working days*, i.e. if your child is born on a Thursday, you have until the following Tuesday at the latest. Otherwise, you cannot register your child's birth without making an application to the courts. The registration should take place at the mairie of the place where your child was born, and the following documents are required:

- the **déclaration de naissance** completed by the hospital, doctor or mid-wife (**sage-femme**)

- official proof of identity (driving licence, carte de séjour) for the person registering the birth

- the mother's **carnet de maternité** (see above)

- the **livret de famille** if you have one (you will only have this if you were married in France)

- your passports (if you and your wife have separate passports).

You should also register your child's birth at your own embassy to ensure the nationality rights of the child for the future. Contact the consular services to find out how to do this.

Child benefit and family allowance

The current levels of Family Allowance are 679 FF per month for two children, 1,548 FF for three children, 2,418 FF for four children and 870 FF per child for five or more children. The amount is increased for children over 10 years old by 191 FF, and by 339 FF for children over 15 years old. To apply for these benefits, you need to register at your local **centre d'allocations familiales.**

In January 1998, the Socialist government provoked outrage by introducing means testing for **allocation familiale**. This takes into account the salaries of both parents if they are working. Further details are available from your local centre.

One Parent Benefit and Child Benefit from the British authorities normally cease if you move abroad permanently. However, if you or your child stay in the UK, you can receive these benefits. Any UK insurance contributions you have paid *may* help in persuading the French authorities to pay you the French **allocations.** More information is available from:

- The Child Benefit Centre, Washington, Newcastle upon Tyne NE88 1BR

- The Family Credit Unit, Customer Service Manager, Room A106B, Government Buildings, Warbreck House, Blackpool FY2 OYF.

Widow's Benefits

Information on Widow's Benefits can be found in Chapter 6.

HELP WITH DISABILITY

There are numerous support groups in France to help disabled or handicapped people and those who care for them. Your doctor should be able to direct you towards the appropriate association. You should also apply to the **bureau de l'aide sociale** of your local mairie for a Disabled Person's Card which will entitle you to certain discounts and assistance.

If you are receiving Severe Disablement Allowance in the UK and you want to go to another EU country, including France, you must contact The Pensions & Overseas Benefits Directorate, Department of Social Security, Tyneview Park, Whitley Road, Benton,

Newcastle upon Tyne NE98 1BA. The decision as to whether you continue to receive this allowance will depend upon your age, how disabled you are, and how long you have lived in the UK.

If you are receiving any form of disability working allowance or carer's allowance, and you move to France, you will not be able to continue receiving British support. Visiting France may also affect your UK allowance. Contact your local benefits authority to see what help they can offer in transferring your rights gained by British National Insurance contributions to the appropriate French authorities.

Services of interest for those with disabilities or handicaps who are living in France include the following:

- **The English Language Library for the Blind** (35 rue Lemercier, 75017 Paris. Tel: 01 42 93 47 57, Tuesday–Thursday 09h00–17h00) supplies a wide variety of recorded books on cassette in return for an annual subscription.

- **France Télécom** provides a range of products called '**Arc-en-Ciel**' (rainbow) which are designed to facilitate communication for the disabled. These include telephones with flashing lights for those with sight disabilities, and a system known as the **boîtier Dialogue** which allows communication via Minitel for the hard-of-hearing or speech-impaired at an increased speed. Ask at France Télécom agencies for details.

- **The French national railways service, SNCF**, offers a variety of travel discounts and arrangements for disabled travellers. These include first class travel at second class tariffs. In some cases the accompanying person will be entitled to travel free. **To qualify for these advantages, apply at the bureau de l'aide sociale of your local mairie for the appropriate card.** Similar offers may be available from other travel companies, so do check.

A list of useful addresses and guides for the disabled is given at the end of this book. Chapter 9 also includes more details about SNCF discounts.

SEXUALLY TRANSMITTED DISEASE

Your nearest hospital will be able to put you in touch with services and clinics for venereal disease. Information in English on HIV and

---

EMERGENCY TELEPHONE NUMBERS IN FRANCE

15 SAMU (ambulance service)
17 Police
18 Sapeurs-Pompiers (fire brigade and ambulance service)

0800 23 13 13 Free drug information service
0800 05 41 41 Free child abuse helpline
0800 306 306 Free helpline for the homeless
0800 840 840 Free AIDS information service in French

01 47 23 80 80 SOS Help
English-language telephone crisis line. Every day 15h00–23h00

01 44 93 16 69 FACTS Helpline
English-language telephone helpline for AIDS and HIV information
and support groups. Monday, Wednesday and Friday 18h00–22h00.

Fig. 9. Emergency telephone numbers in France.

AIDS-related issues is available from FACTS (see Figure 9). For free AIDS information ring the SIDA Infor Service on 0800 840 800 (24 hours a day, 7 days a week).

SERVICES FOR ENGLISH-SPEAKING PATIENTS

Many French doctors do speak some English. However, unless you are reasonably fluent in French and familiar with medical terms, you could experience difficulties, especially if the illness or problem is serious. Help can be found at the following places:

- English-language consulates have lists of English-speaking doctors.

- Private health insurance companies and travellers' associations (e.g. American Express, Automobile Association) often have help-packs which they can provide to their customers before they leave.

- Information on English-language hospitals in France can be found in the Regional Directory at the end of this book.

- A Paris-based English-language group of Alcoholics Anonymous can be contacted on 01 46 34 59 65.

CHECKLIST

1. Have you thought about how you will obtain the medicines which you and your family will especially need?

2. Do you need access to particular medical facilities regularly? Are they available near to the place that you intend to live?

3. Have you applied for the necessary forms to transfer any current benefits you may be receiving?

8
Looking at the
French Education System

The French state education system, like so many other areas of French life at the moment, is going through a period of reflection and potential change at the time of writing. Generally academic levels are very high, and teachers and pupils alike are expected to show a serious commitment to their work.

Crises over educational funding are affecting certain regions of France faster than they can be resolved, and strikes – by teachers, students and even pupils – are quite common. A new report published in April 1998 has called for a reduced workload for staff and **lycée** students, with an emphasis on 'quality rather than quantity', and the introduction of more efficient teaching methods. Amongst younger pupils, the principal concern is to teach increased respect, and to diminish the rather spectacular, but isolated, displays of violence which have occurred in recent years.

THE ACADEMIC YEAR

France very much beats to the rhythm of the academic year. This begins in mid-September with **la rentrée (scolaire)**, and ends in late June. A mid-term break occurs around All Saints Day (**Toussaint**) at the beginning of November, followed by a two-week break for Christmas and New Year. There is then another mid-term break in February, and two weeks for the Easter holidays (not necessarily linked to the date of Easter itself). Holiday dates vary from region to region, so do check your local dates. See also Figure 2 in Chapter 1 for details of the May bank holidays.

THE SCHOOL DAY

In state schools, children attend school from 08h30 to 11h30, and then from 13h30 to 16h30 from Monday to Saturday, with Wednesday and Saturday afternoons free. Variations occur according to the level of education of your child; Wednesdays are completely free for smaller children, whilst Saturday mornings and Wednesdays are obligatory for older children at **lycée**. Some private schools have adopted the more simple five-day week, as have some experimental **collèges**.

ELEMENTARY EDUCATION (AGE 2–6)

School is not compulsory in France for children until they are six years old. Nonetheless, 93 per cent of three-year-old children in France are enrolled in the voluntary **écoles maternelles**. The current schools minister, Ségolène Royal, wants to introduce education for two-year-olds.

Enrolling your child
Enrolment takes place at your local mairie, at the published dates (normally around March), and can be performed as soon as the child reaches the age of two years. At enrolment, you will be informed of the school catchment area you fall into. It is possible to choose another school if you wish by following a typically long procedure. Documents needed to enrol your child are:

- the **livret de famille** (if you were married in France) or a **fiche d'état civile** of the child (see Chapter 3)

- a proof of residence (**justicatif de domicile**) e.g. an electricity bill with your name on

- the **carnet de santé** of your child, proving s/he has received all necessary relevant vaccinations.

Once you have received the enrolment certificate (**certificat d'inscription**) from the mairie, you need to make an appointment straight away with your school director. Children are accepted on a 'first come, first served' basis, with priority for older children. Schooling for children under three years old depends on the availability of places.

The classes offered in the école maternelle are roughly equivalent to Early Learning in the UK for French Year One; the UK Reception Class for Year Two; and UK Year One for the French Year 3 (for five to six-year-old children).

PRIMARY EDUCATION (AGE 6–11)

When your child begins their compulsory education at the age of six, they will enter into the **11ème** classe. The natural progression from now on is to arrive in the **première classe** and then **terminale** (equivalent to Upper Sixth in the UK) at the age of 18 when they will normally take the **baccalauréat** examination equivalent to A-levels.

If your child is already enrolled at an école maternelle, s/he will automatically be enrolled at your local school. Enrolments must take place no later than the month of June preceding your child's entry into the school at the **école elementaire**. For popular schools, the sooner you apply the better your chances are of enrolling your child at the school of your choice. The same processes must be gone through if you wish to choose a school in a different sector. If your child is not already enrolled, you must follow the process outlined above.

In the *écoles élementaires* (for 6–11-year-olds) the course of study may change according to the area you live in. Basically a child is taught to read and write, along with basic maths and a few less academic subjects. As the child grows older, s/he is rigorously taught the grammatic rules of the French language, including spelling and the use of tenses.

A great deal of time is spent learning poetry, which is considered good practice for the child's memory. Sciences of observation will take up about an hour a week depending on the teacher. Most schools now spend a few hours a week on English, arts and crafts, an extra sport, and a computer class. A lot depends on the human and other resources available in a school as to what is offered. A current government project is to encourage the use of the Internet in schools and teaching.

Physical education (PE) usually includes two hours per week of general fitness classes, and at some time or other, all schoolchildren learn how to swim.

SECONDARY EDUCATION (AGE 11–15)

From the *6ème* to the *3ème* (11–15 years old), your children will enter a **collège**. Similar procedures exist for enrolling your child in a *collège* as for other state schools. If you choose a *collège* outside your district, your choice requires further justification than at earlier stages. Acceptance depends on, amongst other factors, the availability of places in the *collège* chosen.

At *collège*, pupils have a different teacher for each subject, and classes generally last about fifty minutes. Maths and French are still the most important subjects, and are really still considered as the keys to a child's success. History and geography are taught as one subject, and physics and natural sciences are each attributed equal importance.

When a pupil enters the *collège* in *6ème*, s/he chooses a foreign language to study – usually English or German. In *4ème* there is the choice of an optional course, usually one of the classical languages of Latin or Greek. Other subjects include crafts, hand drawing, music and PE.

Repeating a year

When a pupil reaches the end of an academic year when they change from one cycle to another – at the end of the *6ème*, *4ème* or *3ème* – the **conseil de classe** ('class board') composed of the teachers concerned decides if the pupil is ready to move on to the next class. If they think not, then they can recommend the pupil to repeat a year (known as **redoublement**).

If you disagree with the decision, you must act swiftly to lodge your complaint (within three days). You will need to see the school director to request an explanation for the decision. However, if you are still not in agreement with the decision, you can force the issue to another 'commission' including other parents, and at which you will be allowed to speak briefly. However, the decision here is final once it is taken.

Planning for the future

In February of the *3ème*, families are requested to fill in a form indicating the proposed career orientation they wish their child to take. Final applications and decisions are taken in May of the *3ème*, with input from the school. At the end of the *3ème* (aged 14–15), pupils take a 'global' examination known as the **brevet**.

The results of this examination, together with the annual report, are used to decide the future education of the pupil. However, it is not an entry examination to *lycée*, but simply a knowledge test for the end of this section of the child's education.

The choices made at this stage affect the type of *lycée* to which your child will next progress, and the sort of qualifications they will leave school with. The choice of *lycées* are:

- **générale et technologique**

- **professionelle.**

The final decision is taken by a small commission, which informs parents at about the end of June which kind of *lycée* their child has been recommended for. More than 25 per cent of pupils currently choose to orientate themselves towards professional life by opting to prepare either a **brevet d'études professionnelle (BEP)** or a **certificat d'aptitude professionelle (CAP)**, both of which are two-year courses at *lycées professionelles*. Normally this will lead to an entry into working life almost immediately after leaving school.

THE FINAL SCHOOL YEARS (AGE 15–18)

The final school years are **seconde, première** and **terminale**. The last of these is when the final **baccalauréat (bac)** examination is taken. For these final years, your child will be educated at a **lycée**. It is here that final choices will be taken which affect the kind of *bac* for which your child will prepare, and consequently, the kind of higher education which they will normally continue with.

Seconde
More than 60 per cent of pupils currently enter the *seconde* in the general/technology classes. This leaves scope for taking final decisions over which type of *bac* to study for. Only those seeking careers in music or dance, or a technical qualification (**brevet de technologie – BT**), have specifically orientated courses. Those preparing either the BEP or CAP (see above) can study a further two years to take a *bac professionnel* before finishing their studies.

Première and terminale
The choice must now be made as to which of the variety of *bacs* your child will study for. The general *bac* leaves the option open for entry into higher education. Other choices will be required if s/he wishes to pursue a vocational course at university. The courses attended in these final years will depend on the option chosen. There are seven compulsory subjects, PE, and two optional subjects.

At the end of *première*, there are written and oral French tests for *bac* candidates. The marks from these are included in the overall success or failure of the candidate. The final examinations are taken in the summer of *terminale*, and results are published very shortly afterwards at around the end of June or beginning of July.

For those who fail the first time, it is possible to retake the *bac*. As it is the key to any form of success in France, as well as entry to higher education, it is highly advisable to do so!

EDUCATION IN ENGLISH

The opportunity for a child to be educated at a French school can be excellent for their future prospects, ensuring that s/he will be bilingual in the future. However, it may also prove frightening and daunting for a child whose command of French is not sufficient. You must also consider the effect upon their education if you will only be living in France short term, and will be returning to your native country and education system.

The options open to you are:

1. Boarding school in the UK or the USA – This may not even be an option, depending on your financial situation, your company's willingness to pay fees, and yours and your child's attitude to boarding school.

2. Private international schools in France – The same financial criteria may affect your decision, as well as accessibility to any such schools.

3. French schools with international sections – These are schools within the state system which normally charge a small fee for schooling in English. These schools work towards the '*Option Internationale*' of the *bac*, and teaching is by native English-speakers.

4. French schools which offer high-level English programmes – Extra hours of education in English from native English-speakers.

5. French schools with European sections – These will normally offer some extra education in English, but not necessarily given by a native English-speaker.

The American and British Schools of Paris (both private schools) follow the national curriculums of their 'home' countries. They would therefore allow your children to continue within the same educational system as they may have known before, according to your own nationality.

The international sections of *lycées* probably offer the best option for those who want their children to benefit from an Anglo-French education at a very reasonable cost. Currently there are about eight British sections in France, and about six American sections. The general rule (which varies between sections) is about four hours per week of English language and literature, and two hours a week of geography and history.

The International option of the *bac* is very highly regarded, and roughly equivalent to S-levels within the British education system. It is therefore a good option for those seeking university entry not only in France, but in other countries too.

More information about native English education in France is available from The English-Language Schools Association France (ELSA-France), 43 rue des Binelles, 92310 Sèvres. Tel: 01 45 34 04 11. Fax: 01 45 34 76 63. E-mail: Association Sis@wanadoo.fr. Refer also to the Regional Directory at the end of this book.

EDUCATIONAL BENEFITS

- **L'aide à la scolarité** – This is available for children at *collège*. It is means-tested, and limited to those who are already receiving another form of family or housing benefit, or benefit for a handicapped adult.

- **L'allocation de rentrée scolaire** – This is available for children aged between six and eighteen years, under the same conditions as above. Each child will automatically be awarded the benefit. Currently the figure is 1,600 FF. The limit of joint income permitted to obtain this benefit rises with the number of children that you have.

Both benefits are administered by the *caisse d'allocations familiales*.

HIGHER EDUCATION

Since 1987, France's student population has grown dramatically. However, there has been no similar growth in funding or facilities. Students tend to go to a university nearest to their homes, partly to keep down costs by continuing to live at home.

The only entrance requirement is normally a pass at *bac*. As a result, there is generally high competition to enrol on the course of your choice at the university of your choice. The university year runs from October until June. About 2,000 FF a year normally covers the costs of enrolment, access to libraries, etc.

The French degree structure
- **Years 1 and 2: DEUG (Diplôme d'Etudes Universitaires Générales)**

– This is the core curriculum course which must be passed (and many fail) before continuing with further study.

- **Year 3: Licence** – This can be passed in most subjects. It is roughly equivalent to a BA or Bsc.

- **Year 4: Maîtrise** – Roughly equivalent to an MA.

- **Year 5: DEA (Diplôme d'Etudes Approfondies)** – A preparatory year for a doctorate.

- The **Doctorate** is the final stage. There is now a limit of four years for completion of the doctoral thesis.

If there is any doubt over the level of your degree, a '**lettre d'équivalence**' can be requested from the Ministère de l'Enseignement et de la Recherche equating your degree to a French degree level.

STUDENT WELFARE

Students have their own *régime* in the *Sécurité Sociale*, for those between 20 and 28 years old. Students from EU countries will need the Form E111 when coming to study in France. They will then need to contact the **Direction des Régimes Spéciaux** of their local university *caisse d'assurance maladie*. There are also student **mutuelles** (complementary health insurance schemes) available.

Housing and other benefits are means-tested on the basis of the income of the student's parents. All students are eligible for limited housing benefit. However, a distinction is made between those who depend solely on their parents for financial support, and those who work their way through their studies. In fact, those who work are worse off in terms of benefits.

The most important place that you will need to find at your particular university is the **CROUS (Centre Régional des Oeuvres Universitaires et Scolaires)**. The CROUS will issue your student card, which will allow you a wide variety of discounts (e.g. travel, museum entrance, etc). The CROUS acts to some extent as a student union would in a British university, in terms of the welfare and general information services it offers.

THE GRANDES ECOLES

As mentioned in Chapter 1, the Grandes Ecoles are the élite higher education institutions (some of which are private), which consistently produce the leaders of French commerce, industry, politics and society in general.

Competition for entry is obviously fierce and very selective. Being a foreigner will probably not help your case, unless you have already attended a top-level university in your own country. However, if you do succeed in graduating from one of these schools, a successful professional life will be almost assured, and a very useful set of future contacts.

THE OPEN UNIVERSITY IN FRANCE

The British distance-learning university, the Open University, has now been operating in France for several years, and has held two degree conferral ceremonies in Paris. All courses are taught in English using proven methods, and cover a wide range of subjects. The obligatory summer schools are also held in France. For further information, write to: Rosemary Pearson, 22 place Georges Pompidou, Boîte 42, 92300 Levallois-Perret. Tel: 01 47 58 53 73. Fax: 01 47 58 55 25.

LANGUAGE SCHOOLS

Private language schools and teachers now abound in French cities and major towns. The quality and value for money that you will receive from these institutions and individuals varies enormously, and you should try to seek local guidance from expatriate groups and colleagues. The Alliance Française is one of the most important teaching associations, with branches nation and worldwide.

Your local **syndicat d'initiative** should be able to provide a list of language schools in your area. Many universities now offer language courses for foreigners. Foreign university students will also normally find that French tuition is included on their timetable.

CHECKLIST

1. What sort of education would your child most benefit from during your time in France?

2. What are the educational facilities available near to your planned new home?

9
Travelling Around

USING YOUR CAR

Driving papers

Officially, it is no longer necessary to exchange your British driving licence (**permis de conduire**) for a French licence if you are resident in France. However, the delay between the announcement of this decision and its application has created an unclear situation. Check with your local préfecture when you arrive to see if you need to exchange your licence, as the official decree appears to be being 'progressively implemented'. Under the old regulations, a British licence had to be exchanged within one year of arrival.

Applications for international driving licences, if necessary, (valid for three years) should be made at your local préfecture. You should note, however, that international licences are not valid in the bearer's country of residence. British citizens visiting France can drive with a UK driving licence.

You must always carry your driving licence with you when driving, as well as the original registration document, and the insurance documents. You must be at least 18 years old to drive in France.

Replacing a lost licence

If you lose your licence or it is stolen, you must report it at the police station nearest to where the incident happened. They will give you a receipt valid for two months, which acts as a temporary licence. During that period go to your local préfecture and request a new licence. Take with you:

- the receipt of your declaration of loss or theft
- some official proof of identity
- the completed form requesting a duplicate licence
- proof of residency (e.g. tenancy agreement, electricity bill, etc.)
- 3 passport-size photos.

It can take three to six weeks to obtain your new licence. You will also have to pay the appropriate fee.

Road rules

The most important thing you do need to remember is that in France you drive on the right! Equally important is the fact that in built-up areas, you must give way to traffic coming from the right – the famous **priorité à droit** rule. In less built-up areas, traffic on main roads has priority over traffic from side roads. The exception to the rule of priority is at roundabouts. Traffic entering the roundabout has priority, *except* when signs such as **cédéz le passage** (give way) or **vous n'avez pas la priorité** are displayed.

Health and safety precautions

- **Seat belts** are obligatory in France, including in the rear of the car if they are installed. You can face an on-the-spot fine if you disobey this rule.

- Random tests are made for **drink-driving** in France, which is a major killer on the roads. The legal limit is now 80mg alcohol per 100ml of blood – not much more than one glass of wine. You may face an on-the-spot fine, a court appearance or a driving ban if you are found guilty. The best solution is not to drink alcohol at all when driving.

- **Speed limits** are reduced in bad weather. Generally on toll motorways (**autoroutes à péage**) the maximum speed is 130kph. The minimum speed in the outside (overtaking) lane is 80kph during daylight on flat roads with good visibility. For dual carriageways and toll-free motorways, the maximum speed limit is 110kph; for other 'departmental' roads the limit is 90kph; and for roads in built-up areas the limit is 50kph.

- Cars made in the UK and Ireland must adjust their **headlights** in order not to dazzle on-coming traffic. Headlight converters made from pre-cut black masking tape must be fitted over the headlights. If another driver flashes his headlights at you it is to indicate that he has priority and that you should give way.

- If you **break down**, try to move the car to the side of the road and flash your hazard warning lights. The red warning triangle should be placed 30m behind your car (100m on motorways). Emergency phones (**postes d'appel d'urgence**) are at 4km intervals on main roads, and every 2km on motorways.

- If you have an **accident**, you should call the police immediately by dialling 17. The ambulance service will also be alerted if necessary. You and the other parties must complete and exchange an accident statement form (**constat à l'amiable**) and exchange insurance details. If possible, persuade witnesses (**témoins**) to remain and make statements.

IMPORTING A CAR

You can import a car for up to six months in one year without completing customs formalities. A new or used car on which VAT (TVA in France) has already been paid in another EU country can be imported into France by a French resident free of French VAT.

Otherwise, VAT is payable *immediately* upon entry into France. You can pay at the point of importation or at your local tax office. You will then be issued with a customs certificate (**Certificat de Douane 846A**) permitting you to register the vehicle in France. The same form will also be required even if VAT has already been paid, to prove that this obligation has been met.

REGISTERING A CAR IN FRANCE

Imported vehicles must be registered in France within three months of entry. To do this, you must contact the local **Direction Régionale de l'Industrie, de la Recherche et de l'Environnement (DRIRE)**. They will provide a checklist of documents required, which are:

1. Proof of origin of the vehicle or certificate of sale.

2. The foreign registration document.

3. The customs certificate 846A (see above).

4. A manufacturer's certificate of construction. This is available from a local car dealer, the French importer, or the manufacturer. *Officially* it is no longer required, but it may be asked for. It can also be very expensive.

5. A completed request for a registration card form (**Demande de Certificat d'Immatriculation d'un Véhicule**). These are available from the Préfecture, or the Préfecture de Police, or the local mairie in Paris.

6. A technical test certificate if your vehicle is more than four years old. All vehicles over this age are subject to regular testing every two years.

The next step after sending these documents to the DRIRE is an appointment at the local vehicle control centre (**Inspecteur des Mines**). After checking that your car meets French construction and use regulations, you will receive a certificate from DRIRE which will finally allow you to apply for the registration certificate (**Certificat d'Immatriculation** – more normally known as a **carte grise**). This happens at the Préfecture, or the Préfecture de Police, or local mairie in Paris.

Once you finally receive your car registration, new number plates must be installed within 48 hours. They can be made up and fitted at local garages for a small fee. The last two numbers of your new registration will refer always to the département in which the car is registered.

Registering a new car
You have 15 days in which to register a newly purchased car. You will need a new form to apply for a new **carte grise**, the certificate of sale, the technical certificate from the **Inspections des Mines**, proof of identity (e.g. carte de séjour), and proof of residence less than three months old (e.g. electricity or telephone bill in your name).

Registering a second-hand car
Once again you have 15 days in which to register. Vehicles less than ten years old cost the same to register as new vehicles; those which are more than ten years old cost half as much to register. You will need proof of identity and proof of residence (as above), and the **carte grise barrée** (old registration document of the car) supplied by the former owner.

Cars more than four years old must also have the necessary technical certificate dating from less than six months before the purchase. You also need a **certificat de situation administrative** supplied by the seller.

Moving home
Even if you stay in the same département, you must change the address on your **carte grise**. This is free, and can be done immediately at the local mairie or préfecture, by presenting a new proof of residence and your **carte grise**. If you fail to do this, you

could face a fine of 600 FF.

Replacing your carte grise
If you lose your carte or it is stolen, you must report it to the police. You will be issued with a temporary document which will allow you to use your car. It will also allow you to apply for a new carte. You will need proof of identity, proof of residence, the receipt of your police statement of loss, the form requesting a duplicate carte, and the necessary technical certificate for vehicles more than four years old.

Selling your car
If you decide to sell your car once you have moved to France, you must supply the following documents to the buyers before the sale is complete and legal:

1. The **certificat de vente** – it is your responsibility to obtain this from the prefecture or sous préfecture.

2. The **carte grise barrée** ie 'crossed-out'. You must write across the carte in indelible ink **'vendue le_____'** (sold on_____) and fill in the date. You must then sign the amended carte.

3. If the car is more than four years old, a technical certificate dated less than six months before the date of the sale proving that the car is roadworthy (see above).

4. A **certificat de situation administrative** – to obtain this, go to your local préfecture with your carte grise. You will need to submit the registration number of the vehicle, the model, and the power of the engine. The certificat will certify that there are no oustanding fines relating to the vehicle.

Within 15 days of the sale of the car, you must hand in the second copy of the certificat de vente at the préfecture at which it was previously registered.

INSURANCE, FUEL AND POLLUTION CONTROLS

Insurance
Fully comprehensive insurance is advisable to cover the costs of breakdown or accidents. Third party motor insurance for unlimited liability is compulsory in France. You will need to shop around to find the best policies and prices.

A useful organisation which has been created to deal with problems arising out of car insurance disputes or lack of insurance cover for motor vehicles is Fonds de Garantie Automobiles. They have offices in Marseille and just outside Paris. Contact details are given at the end of this book in the Useful Addresses.

Tax

Tax disks (**vignette**) can be purchased at either the tabac or the local tax office, and should be displayed in the usual way on the inside of the windscreen.

Fuel

Garages are placed at intervals of 24km along all motorways. Leaded petrol is now sold only in one grade (**essence super**). Unleaded is sold in two grades: **essence sans plomb**, and **super sans plomb**. The minimum quantity that you can buy is five litres. Diesel (**gazole**) is cheaper and readily available. **Faites le plein, s'il vous plaît** means 'Fill her up, please'.

Pollution controls

In recent years, pollution has become a major problem in Paris and other major cities, especially in the summer months. To combat this problem, regulations are enforced each year (or sometimes simply threatened), whereby you can only drive on alternate days. This depends on the last two numbers before the letters in a number plate.

On one day, only even numbers (**pairs**) will be allowed to drive; the next day it will be the turn of the uneven numbers (**impairs**). Listen out for warnings on the TV and radio.

TRAVELLING BY TRAIN

The state-owned railway company, the **Société Nationale des Chemins de Fer (SNCF)**, operates the most extensive train network in western Europe, with over 21,000 miles of track. The high-speed **TGV** (**Train Grand Vitesse** – literally 'very high speed') trains have been successfully exported to other countries on the basis of their success in France. A new high-speed link has at last been announced to Strasbourg, which will finally link the east of France to the capital and the rest of the country within the extensive TGV network.

Buying your ticket

If you go to one of the principal railway stations, look to see if one of the counters (**guichets**) has a British flag displayed in the window. If so, the ticket seller will (notionally) speak some English and will be able to help you. A one-way ticket is an **aller-simple**. A return ticket is an **aller-retour**.

Tickets are valid for two months from the date of purchase. Once you have validated (**composté**) your ticket by punching it in the orange box at the entrance to the platform, it will be valid for only 24 hours from the date and time punched on the ticket.

> **Always remember to validate your ticket *before* entering the train. A non-validated ticket could lead to a hefty fine. This also applies on local suburban SNCF trains.**

Making reservations

Tickets can be reserved on most trains, and **must** be reserved on all TGV trains. A small reservation fee (about 20 FF) will be levied, but the exact sum depends on the time and category of the train, and of your ticket. Reservations include the choice of first or second class, smoking or non-smoking, and window or aisle seats.

You can either make your reservation in person, or over the telephone by calling the appropriate station, or even by Minitel. Tickets reserved over the phone or by Minitel and paid for by credit card must be collected within 48 hours from an SNCF station. You can also use the automatic ticket machines in the major stations to make reservations, at the same time as buying your ticket. All reservations will include a carriage number and seat number.

Choosing when to travel

There are basically two tariff periods, blue and white. Blue is the reduced tariff period for off-peak travel, and white is the opposite. The tariff you pay depends on which period you begin your journey in, regardless of whether it ends in a different period. Check which period your journey falls in before buying your ticket and making your final arrangements.

In peak holiday periods – **Toussaint** at the beginning of November, Christmas, the spring school holidays, the May bank holidays, and in July and August – you should definitely make reservations on all main-line journeys to avoid the discomfort of three hours standing up in a French train corridor.

Reduced price tickets

The SNCF offer a wide number of interesting reductions available to young and old individuals and families. Leaflets concerning these offers, partly printed in English, are available in all main-line SNCF stations. The most complete guide (in French) is the **Guide du Voyageur** available free in all main stations.

- If you reserve your ticket no later than 30 days before your departure you can make a significant saving on the ticket price (**Prix découvert J30**). If you reserve no later than eight days before departure, significant savings are still offered (**Prix découvert J8**). Reductions depend upon which tariff period you choose to travel in.

- If you make a return journey accompanied by another person – whether you arc related or not – you can save up to 25 per cent on the cost of your journey (**Prix découvert à deux**).

- If you have at least three children, of whom at least one is under 18 years old, you qualify for the **Carte Famille Nombreuse**. This offers very significant savings, up to 75 per cent of the price of standard tickets.

- The two **Kiwi** cards offer cheap travel for children under 16, and for those accompanying them. Adults are included in the deal, and do not need to be related to the holder of the card. The **Jeune Voyager Service** arranges the appropriate care of children travelling alone.

- The new **Carte 12–25 ans** offers reduced travel rates to those people who fall within that age group.

- The Annual Holiday Ticket (**billet de congé annuel**) is available to those in and out of work, and also to retired people. There are certain conditions attached to availability for the unemployed. The reduction offered is 25 per cent.

- Group travel (10 people and over) has a tariff structure linked to the size of your group.

- For **les seniors** (over 60), the two **Carte Vermeil** cards operate in a very similar way to the **Kiwi** cards for **les juniors**. Savings are in the region of 20–50 per cent.

- A guide is available for those with handicaps or mobility difficulties. Ask for the free **Guide du voyageur à mobilité réduite**.

- If your train is late arriving, and is a **Grande Ligne** train, you are entitled to be reimbursed 25 per cent of the ticket price for a delay of 30–60 minutes, and 50 per cent for delays over an hour.

Travelling at night

Three options exist for those who wish or need to travel overnight.

1. Reclining seats (**sièges à dossiers inclinables**) are available in certain trains in second class carriages. You should reserve these seats in advance (currently 20 FF).

2. The famous bunk-beds (**couchettes**) are available in first class (four to a cabin) and second class (six to a cabin). The current cost is 90 FF, and reservations should be made.

3. Sleeping compartments (**les voitures-lits**) are also available on certain trains: individually in first class, and for two to three people in second class. Enquire at main stations for further details.

No matter which option you choose, take great care over money and important personal belongings on night trains.

Transporting animals

Cats and dogs accompanying children using a **Kiwi** pass (see above) travel free. Larger domestic pets are charged at about 50 per cent of the price of a second class ticket. Small dogs, less than 6kg, transported in a bag or basket, cost a maximum of 31 FF to transport. One thing to remember is that if another traveller objects to your pet, you may have to change seats or even carriages.

Transporting vehicles

Motorail is a European network of over one hundred services within France and Europe which allows you to transport your car or motorbike by train. In the UK and Ireland, you should contact Rail Europe UK (see Useful Addresses at the end of this book) to make advance bookings which are strongly recommended. If you book in France, you will be given a **guide du voyage** containing practical information at the same time as you receive your travel documents.

Vehicles are generally loaded about one hour before departure, and are normally available for collection about half an hour after arrival. Loading and collection times will be marked on your tickets.

In France, both services are performed by the relevant staff. Motorbikes are always loaded and unloaded by the driver.

Generally, loading and collection take place in the station where the passenger boards the train. If it does not, a free bus (**navette**) will transport you between the loading or collection point, and your place of departure or arrival. A free guide *Auto/Train* is available from main SNCF stations. For information on Eurotunnel services, contact a travel agent or the company itself.

CYCLING

Local tourist offices (**syndicats d'initiatives**) will be able to tell you where you can hire bikes. It is also possible to hire bikes at over 200 SNCF stations in much the same way that cars are hired (i.e. collect at one station and deposit at another).

For short journeys, you can put your cycle in the luggage van for free. For longer journeys, it needs to be registered, and you should really send it a few days in advance. A leaflet available at SNCF stations gives the list of stations and prices for the bike hire service.

AIR TRAVEL

The national airline, Air France, operates worldwide. The two principal airports are Roissy-Charles-de-Gaulle and Orly, just outside Paris. The airports in Bordeaux, Lyon, Marseille, Nantes, Nice, Strasbourg and Toulouse all have direct scheduled international flights.

There are also a number of smaller regional airports which are served by some smaller companies, and by Air Inter (a subsidiary of Air France). The new EU regulations have obliged France to open internal air-routes to foreign companies, and the market should develop further in the next few years.

DUTY-FREE

Up until 30 June 1999, you will still be able to profit from duty-free shopping at airports, on ferries, at ports, on planes and at the entry to the Channel Tunnel. The total value of your purchases must not exceed a limit of 600 FF. If you are travelling outside the EU area, you will still have the right to buy duty-free products within the defined limits.

TRAVELLING BY BOAT

For details of travel by **ferry**, to the UK, Ireland or Corsica, you should contact your local travel agent. The choice of companies and ports for the UK covers most of the northern French coast.

In Paris, the regional transport authority now operates a **Bat-o-bus** in the summer months on the Seine.

Permits

Neither sailing boats nor motor boats with motors less than 6CV require driving permits. However, for **coastal navigation**, three types of permit exist.

- **La Carte Mer**. Required if you intend to sail a boat with a motor between 6 and 50CV. This permits you to undertake daytime sailing, within a limit of about 9km. The test is a mix of theory and practical, requiring about five or six theory sessions and one or two practical sessions before the test.

- **Le Permis Mer Cotier**. For boats with motors over 50CV. This permit also covers night-time sailing, but within the same geographical limit. A similar style of test must be passed as for La Carte Mer.

- **Le Permis Mer Hauturier**. This allows all forms of sailing. To take the test for this permit, you must enrol in a boat school. The cost includes a **timbre fiscal** (fiscal stamp) of 250 FF for enrolment on the course, and one of 400 FF for the issue of the certificate. Both stamps must be applied to the application form.

Further details are available on all of these permits from the Bureau de la Navigation de Plaisance, 3 place Fontenoy, 75007 Paris. Tel: 01 44 49 80 00.

Permits are also required if you intend to take advantage of France's extensive network of **rivers**, if the boat is more than 5m long or travels at more than 20kph.

- **Permis C**. Also known as the **coches de plaisance**, this allows you to sail a boat less than 15m long at less than 20kph. A theory test must be passed.

- **Permis S**. Also known as the **bateaux de sport**, this allows you to sail a boat less than 15m but which travels at more than 20kph.

The test is both theoretical and practical for this permit.

- **PP.** Also known as **péniches de plaisance**, this permits you to sail a boat more than 15m long. The test is composed of the same elements as the Permis S.

To enrol for any of these permits, contact a boat school.

A permit is not required on certain waterways if you decide to take a **barge holiday** in France. Unless you possess the Permis PP, you must hire a boat of less than 15m at a speed of less than 20kph. The hirer will give you a **carte de plaisance** for the length of your stay on the boat, which will be your sailing permit.

COACH TRAVEL

Two coach operators run services from the UK to France. City Sprint (a partner of the Hoverspeed ferry company) runs a service from London to Paris. Eurolines offers a much more extensive coverage of France with over 50 destinations. Contact details are given at the end of this book.

CHECKLIST

1. If you are bringing your car to France, have you collected together all the necessary paperwork?

2. What means of travel will you need to use most frequently when you are in France? How easy is it to access these from where you are planning to live?

10
Enjoying Your Leisure Time

France is the land of the **bonviveur**, literally the 'good-liver'. A great deal of importance is placed upon the pursuit of leisure. Relaxing, building bonds with family and friends, and exploring new activities are all ingrained elements of the French way of life. A great deal of stress is laid upon encouraging **solidarité** between ages and social classes. One of the new super-ministries of the Socialist government is the ministry of employment and solidarity.

ENTERTAINING AND SOCIAL LIFE

Enjoying French dinner parties
Dinner parties in France are normally held at about 20h00–21h00. Try to be reasonably on time so as not to spoil a carefully prepared meal by leaving it to simmer longer than intended. Written invitations should be acknowledged by written replies. Normally, a French dinner consists of the following elements:

- starter (**entrée**) normally accompanied by white wine

- main course (**plat**) accompanied by red wine, unless white wine is appropriate

- cheese *before* dessert, served either by itself or with a light salad

- dessert perhaps accompanied by a special dessert wine

- coffee, served at the table; this may or may not be followed by liqueurs.

Very grand dinners will have a sorbet between each course, to clear the taste buds. It is not advisable to take wine as a gift for your hostess. French people are generally knowledgeable about wine, and will normally have carefully selected what they wish to serve with a particular meal. If you take a gift of wine, it should be good quality and French. Non-French wine is viewed, at best, with caution. Gifts of wine will almost certainly be placed in the store, and served on a later occasion at which you will not be present. A bottle of Champagne is a good present, which need not be expensive. This can also be laid down in a cellar, or chilled during dinner and served with dessert. Flowers are cumbersome for a hostess when she is about to serve dinner. For foreigners, bringing a product or gift from your country is an original idea, and provides a talking point at the table. A small box of good chocolates is also another popular gift, which can be purchased from specialist shops, or even at the **boulangerie**.

If you do not wish to drink alcohol, mineral water is almost always available at French tables and in all restaurants. Smoking is very prevalent in France, and rules regarding smoking at the table – and even between courses – will vary according to the hosts and the company you keep. As with many table manners, it is very much a game of 'follow my leader'. If you object to somebody smoking beside you, a discreet request rather than a loud haughty lecture will achieve the effect you require.

You may well find a rack or block beside your plate, which is a knife or fork rest. In France, it is quite common to keep the same cutlery throughout several courses. Bread is normally in plentiful supply on French tables, and should be broken with your hands, not cut with a knife. Butter is not normally served with bread.

Whilst business associates may well be invited to dinner, there is rarely 'shop talk' at the table. Conversation is more likely to revolve around new films, exhibitions, current events – and probably you as a foreigner in France. French dinner parties, like any other, can either be insufferably formal or very relaxed. If you do not know the rest of the party well, remember that the French are generally conservative and dress accordingly. The fading custom of sending thank you notes is nonetheless greatly appreciated, and will probably ensure your popularity with your new friends.

Formality and etiquette are part of the French fascination with rules and regulations. If you are worried about making gaffs (**faux pas**), then invest in one of the many etiquette guides available.

Eating out in restaurants

Finding good restaurants which offer value for money can be difficult. Restaurant guides can be useful, but recommendations from locals are often the most reliable.

Generally, restaurants offer a choice between meals at a fixed price chosen from a menu or **formule**, or allow you to choose from the whole menu, which is known as eating **à la carte**. The formule is normally more economical, and generally involves a selection of the dishes offered in the menu. It may be a starter (**entrée**) and main course (**plat**), or a main course and dessert, or all three. A small jug of wine (**pichet**) is also sometimes included. Alternatively, you can ask for a jug of water (**une carafe d'eau**) which is free. Mineral water must be paid for.

Note: Some restaurants will only offer a lunchtime set menu (**formule du midi**). Be careful to check this before you set out for the restaurant in the evenings, especially if you are on a limited budget.

The menu should always indicate if service is included (**service compris**). This may affect your decision as to whether to leave a tip, especially in expensive restaurants. If you order a meat dish, depending on the meat you will be asked how you like it cooked – **quelle cuisson**?

- **saignant** – rare

- **à point** – medium rare

- **bien cuit** – well done

The French like their meat cooked very rare compared to the British, so you should perhaps overcompensate if you do not like rare meat.

Foreign and regional food

The choice of restaurants available will depend on your location. Non-French food is widely available, and as in the UK the choice reflects France's colonial past. Vietnamese and North African food (**couscous**) is popular, and Chinese and Italian food is fairly widely available. In Paris, the two 'Chinatowns' are to be found in Belleville and near the Place d'Italie. Indian food is rarer, although in Paris once again you should go to the Passage Brady near Strasbourg-St Denis. British cooking is still eyed with suspicion and/or mirth in France, and there are very few British restaurants.

What you will find in France is a great choice of restaurants offering regional specialities. It can be great fun when visiting a new area to try not only the local cheese and wine, but also the local dish. Some are now universal, and you will find **bœuf Bourguignonne** (Burgundy beef stew), for instance, available everywhere.

Fast food and take-aways

Fast food is widely available now in France, and major international chains have outlets in most principal towns and cities. Chinese and Indian take-aways do not exist, but home-delivery pizza services are widespread.

Cafés and pubs

Cafés are one of the great traditions of French society, ranging from the high-brow literary *salons* of St Germain des Prés in Paris to scruffy street-corners, and encompassing every style in between.

Drinking at the counter (**comptoir**) is cheaper than at a table (**en salle**) or on a terrace (**en terrasse**). The same rules apply in cafés to ordering alcohol as to ordering coffee or tea. Exploring the local cafés and finding one that suits you, where you can while away half an hour with the newspaper, a book or friends for the price of a coffee, is another of the joys of France. In main cities, some cafés also become centres of nightlife.

Those cafés which display a red **tabac** sign also double as tobacconists, offering a wide range of products at the cigarette counter (e.g. phone cards or fiscal stamps). Many also offer a **service restauration** at least at lunchtime, with sandwiches and hot meals available. Some of the terms for these meals you will need to know include:

- **Croque-monsieur** – ham and cheese toasted sandwich.

- **Croque-madame** – as above, but with a fried egg served on top.

- **Chèvre-chaud** – hot goat's cheese normally served on toast, with a small mixed salad. Either a starter or a main course.

- **Francfort-frites** – Frankfurter sausage and chips. Sausages such as **Saucisse de Toulouse** are more like a Cumberland sausage and will be served with other vegetables and a sauce.

- **Garnis avec...** – served with: chips (**frites**), boiled potatoes (**pommes vapeur**), fried/roast potatoes (**pommes sautés**), pasta (**pâtes**).

- **Salade** – be careful here. In French this can mean lettuce, which may be all you receive, or, for instance, you may receive a **salade de tomates** (a plate of sliced tomatoes). A **salade mixte** will be a side salad of lettuce plus perhaps chicory (**endives**) and tomatoes. Salads which are served as main courses will normally have a list of their ingredients.

- **Omelettes** are normally also available in a variety of styles and content.

Pubs are now increasingly popular in France, and there are over 60 Irish pubs across France in the principal cities, most notably Paris. However, you should note that whilst they appear to be like English and Irish pubs, the prices are very much higher. Do *not* walk in and offer a round of drinks to your friends unless you are prepared, or feeling very generous!

A pint normally costs about 60 FF in a pub, and spirits are also about 40–60 FF per glass. The cost of a glass of wine will depend on its size and quality. The standard French person will drink a half-pint (**demie**) of whatever is on tap (**pression**). This is one local custom you should take up quickly!

Cabarets and clubs

In the major cities, you will find nightlife for which the French have been famous for generations centred around cabarets and night-clubs. In Paris, the 'Folies-Bergères', the 'Lido', the 'Crazy Horse' and the 'Moulin-Rouge' continue to offer high-class – but expensive – entertainment, with a champagne dinner served whilst grand musical shows are performed. Smaller cabarets are also very popular, allowing singers and comedians to perform in a more intimate atmosphere.

Nightclubs, almost by definition, fall in and out of fashion very rapidly and regularly. You should check the style of a club by using a guide, or by asking somebody whom you know already goes to the club. Styles vary widely, even at the same club, depending on the day of the week. The trendiest Paris nightclubs have a very exclusive door-policy, so swot up in advance on what to wear and how to act.

French nightlife gets going much later than in the UK. Bars generally close at 02h00, and nightclubs will generally start to fill up from about 01h00, and then stay open until dawn. The entry price may include one drink (**une consommation**), but after that be prepared for high prices.

Parties

Cocktail parties usually begin about 19h00, and will last for a couple of hours. Informality over the time of arrival may not be matched by informality over dress, and you should try to find out roughly what is expected of you.

If you decide to organise a more traditional British-style party, do not expect your French guests to bring a bottle with them. In France, the host traditionally provides all the requirements for an evening's entertainment. One way to get around this is to call a party a **soirée à l'anglaise**, literally a British evening, and gently explain the bring-a-bottle concept to your French guests. You should warn both neighbours and the concierge that you will be organising a party, and post polite notes in French in the entrance hall of your building apologising in advance for any inconvenience caused.

Encourage your guests to leave quietly, and be careful of the level of noise. The police may be asked to intervene at rowdy parties after 22h00. Your neighbours will normally be forgiving if you make an excuse such as 'It's my birthday'. However – remember you only have one birthday a year!

BIRTHS, MARRIAGES AND DEATHS

Although these are not leisure activities, it is appropriate to know a few of the social customs of the hatching, matching and despatching 'business' which still thrives in republican France. Obviously there is no Court Circular page in French newspapers, but both *Le Figaro* and *Le Monde* carry social announcements, as well as *Libération* to a lesser extent. The choice of paper depends entirely on the class pretensions and politics of those concerned.

Births
Births (**naissances**) are often announced not only by cards as in the UK but also by a small advertisement in one of the papers named above. Typically, a birth announcement will be roughly translated as, 'Marie and Pierre are pleased to announce the arrival of their new sister Jeanne' followed by the name and address of the parents.

Infant baptisms are heavily on the decline in France. For Catholic families, they normally take place during the Parish Mass on Sunday mornings, and will be followed by a family lunch. Coloured sugared almonds (**dragées**) are often distributed, pink for girls and blue for boys.

Marriages
No religious wedding ceremony may take place in France until a civil marriage has first been performed by the mayor at the town hall. This applies to all religions and denominations. If a large religious ceremony is to follow, then normally only close family and

friends will attend the wedding at the **mairie**. However, many people choose to stick to civil marriage. Being invited to be a **témoin** (witness) is an honour equivalent to being a bridesmaid or usher.

Wedding lists are very popular in France, and are an easy way of dealing with the problem of presents. The style of the wedding is, of course, entirely personal to the couple, and may range from the unusual to the strictly traditional. A traditional Catholic wedding will take place in the course of a Nuptial Mass, normally in the bride's home parish.

As with British weddings, French weddings can be the occasion for a great show of finery. As ever in France, be careful to find out as much about the dress code expected as possible. The wedding invitation may well read like a genealogy of the couple, with grandparents and parents of both sides listed.

The French tradition in wedding receptions is the opposite of the British. Everybody is invited after the wedding to the **vin d'honneur**, to toast the couple's health and happiness. However after that the reception is limited, ranging from a seated dinner (**dîner placé**), to a **soirée dansante** (dance). If you are lucky enough to be invited to a French aristocratic wedding, this will normally take place at the family château.

Deaths

Generally you will receive a **faire-part** (card announcing a death), including the same genealogical list as you would find on a wedding invitation – only longer. For instance, a *faire-part* announcing the death of a grandmother would begin with her spouse, include any surviving brothers and sisters and their spouses, and then move on to mention each child and their children, sometimes each by name.

The French are very attached to the tradition of writing to express condolence. The faire-part will announce when and where the funeral is to take place, whether donations should be made in place of flowers, and whether it is a 'family only' affair (**dans la plus stricte intimité**).

At a French Requiem Mass, each mourner will be invited to take part in the ritual of absolution, the **absolut** (sprinkling of holy water), as a final farewell. This is not obligatory if it contradicts your own faith. If you do wish to participate, move at the instruction of the undertaker, and then 'follow the leader'.

Burial is still much the most common end for French men and women, and cremations are rare. It should be noted that French crematoria are to say the least much less 'user-friendly' than British ones.

THE PERFORMING ARTS

France is traditionally very generous in state patronage of the arts. The result is a rich variety in the performing arts, which is by no means concentrated uniquely in the major cities. Tourist information centres will be able to tell you what forthcoming productions and events are planned in your own area.

Music

Regional festivals and the system of **conservatoires** (music academies) ensure a broad availability of music in the more populated areas. Paris naturally has a high concentration of fine concert halls, but there is a very important musical life outside the capital also. Each summer, for instance, Radio France organises a classical music festival in Montpelier.

Popular music concerts take place all over France, with world-renowned singers touring. The **Printemps de Bourges** festival is a major jamboree and recruitment session in central France for rock fans and recording artistes.

It should be noted that the English-language expatriate communities are very well-served by semi-professional musicians in and around Paris. The main bases for these groups and individuals are the American Cathedral and St George's Anglican Church (see the Regional Directory for address details).

Opera

Opera flourishes in Paris, not only in the new Bastille Opéra House, but also at the Opéra-Comique, and sometimes also at the old Paris Opéra (the **Palais Garnier**), and in other theatres such as the Théâtre Chatelet. There are also important opera houses in Bordeaux, Nice and Montpelier (where there are in fact two opera houses). Both traditional and modern operas are included in their repertoires.

The Paris Ballet is now housed at the grand old Opéra-Garnier, and provides a full programme each season. Visiting ballets also regularly appear in Paris.

Theatre

The theatre in Paris especially thrives, with many small theatres offering the chance for new actors and productions to appear before the public. The most famous French theatre is the **Comédie-Française**, which now has three theatres. There are also occasional performances in English in Paris, most notably at the Odéon and the Shakespeare Garden in the Bois de Boulogne.

Cinema

Cinema is one of the great passions of the French. Along with the theatre festival at Avignon, the film festival at Cannes each year is a major international cultural highlight. Films in English with French sub-titles are widely shown and are marked **v.o.** (**version originale**); **v.f.** (**version française**) means that films have been dubbed. There is also an American Film Festival at Deauville and a British film festival at Dinard each year.

GALLERIES AND HISTORICAL MONUMENTS

France is home to arguably the world's greatest museum, the Louvre, which is the centre-piece of the cultural jewel which is Paris. A good guidebook to Paris (there are hundreds to choose from) will be a worthwhile investment. However, you should remember that there is a hidden wealth of art galleries, museums and historical monuments across France.

From the gothic cathedrals of Amiens, Rheims and Rouen in the north to the painter Chagall's hideaway at St Paul-de-Vence in the south, via the Baroque splendours of Versailles, the châteaux of the Loire Valley and the restored medieval ramparts of Carcassone, France is packed with fascinating and well-preserved historical monuments.

The municipal art galleries (**musées des beaux-arts**) of Lille and Rouen are particularly fine, and there is an important art gallery (the **Musée Fabre**) in Montpelier also. Driving through the valleys of the Dordogne region, you will come across ruined castles, and across France you will find many ancient shrines around which grew up often well-preserved medieval towns.

Each time you intend to visit a new city or region, buy yourself a regional guidebook if you can. This will allow you to get the best out of even a short stay. The best series of guidebooks for France remains the **green Michelin guides**, which are also available in English.

SPORT

As with so many other activities, the French are nothing if not passionate about sport. A French player or team who wins a competition in no matter what discipline can be certain of a hero's welcome on the Champs-Elysées when they return to France, as well as endless hours of television coverage – until or unless they are knocked out of a competition, when TV interest noticeably evaporates.

Details of local facilities – which are widespread and generally of a high standard – can be obtained from the local **mairie** or **syndicat d'initiative**. Sport is very well regarded in France as a means of social interaction, and some of the poorest and most troubled areas have the highest sporting take-up rates.

Soccer is one of the national obsessions, and will be even more so after the World Cup hosted by France in 1998. To celebrate this occasion, the French have offered themselves a magnificent new stadium just north of Paris. The leading clubs are Paris-St Germain (PSG) and Olympic Marseille (OM), although there are regional clubs all over France who participate in national and international leagues.

Rugby is another national obsession, especially beating the British whenever possible. This is most notably during the Five Nations tournament each year. Rugby is particularly strong in the south west around Toulouse, and in central France near Brive-le-Gaillard (literally 'Brive the strong').

Tennis is another favourite pastime, encouraged by the French climate. The Roland Garros competition just outside Paris, and the Paris Open Tennis championships, rival Wimbledon in drawing the great names to play. **Basketball** is another popular sport, and France's geography also favours **water sports**, from swimming to surfing to water-skiing. If you enjoy sailing, be sure to read Chapter 9 (section on **permits**) before setting sail from the coasts of France.

Winter sports have always been a French speciality due to the mountainous Italian, Spanish and Swiss borders. The ski resorts are very well developed, and often full at peak holiday periods. In the summer months, **mountaineering** and **hiking** are also popular pastimes. **Cycling** dominates news coverage for at least several weeks each year when the Tour de France weaves its way across the country and into Paris. Cross-country cycling is increasingly popular.

Racing enthusiasts will find plenty to please them in France. Deauville and Paris are both well known centres for horse-racing. The great races each year are the **Prix de l'Arc de Triomphe** at Longchamps on the first weekend in October (the occasion of a British mini-invasion for the French equivalent of The Derby), and the **Prix de Diane** at Chantilly in June (which is really the equivalent of the Ascot Gold Cup, with lots of silly hats included).

HOBBIES

Joining a club or society can be a good way of meeting people and making friends in your own neighbourhood. It can also be a good opportunity to practise or improve your French. The Regional Directory at the end of this book will give you indications as to how to contact clubs and societies in your area which are specifically for foreign residents. Otherwise the local mairie will also be able to point you in the right direction for finding groups such as ramblers (**randonneurs**) or wine-tasters, or indeed whatever your own particular interest might be.

If you enjoy fishing, you should note that you will need a licence (**carte de pêche**). There is no examination for this, but you do have to pay. For further details contact the Union Nationale de Pêche, 17 rue Bergère, 75009 Paris. Tel: 01 48 24 96 00. A junior card exists for children under 16. There are also cards valid for 15 days for holidaymakers.

VOLUNTEERING

Another way of meeting people is to join a charitable association. Giving a little of your time as a **bénévole** (volunteer) can make a lot of difference to the well-being of both the charity and the people it seeks to help.

You may initially find that your linguistic abilities will limit your options for action within a French charity. However, there is always a need for people at all levels and of all abilities. In larger associations, you may find that as an English-speaker you are particularly useful in making contact with other similar associations outside France.

The largest charities in France are those helping people affected by AIDS (**SIDA** in French), cancer research, the Red Cross (**Croix-Rouge**) and charities such as Abbé Pierre's '**Emmaus**' Project for housing assistance for poor families. One of the most well-known charities is the **Restos du Cœur**, which runs mobile soup-kitchens helping 'down-and-outs'.

Three English-language charity projects based in Paris also rely entirely on volunteer helpers in all areas of their work, and you could consider helping them:

- The English Language Library for the Blind, 35 rue Lemercier, 75017 Paris. Tel: 01 42 93 47 57.

- SOS Help – the English-language telephone crisis line, linked to The Samaritans. Tel: 01 47 23 80 80.

- FACTS – the English-language AIDS support and information service, 190 boulevard Charonne, 75020 Paris. Tel: 01 44 93 16 32.

GOING ON HOLIDAY

In 1996, France was the most visited country in the world, with 62.4 million tourists. As a foreigner in France, you will probably want to take advantage of the wonderful opportunities all around you to explore your new home. This need not be expensive, and can be easily done using public transport as well as private vehicles. The French have a sometimes curious 'herd-instinct' and tend to leave the cities in droves to 'escape' each other, only to find that the resorts are full of their compatriots doing likewise.

If you can take a break out of high season, you will enjoy it more, it will probably be cheaper, and you will certainly have more choice over accommodation. Chapter 9 includes details of some offers available from the SNCF train service. The **Gîtes** system (small country properties) offers the opportunity for self-catering in pleasant surroundings. Hotels range from the cheap and cheerful Formule 1 outside major towns, to the luxurious **Relais Châteaux**, with a wide range in between.

Planning your holiday
- Check your dates – do they coincide with the school holidays?

- Check what the weather is normally like at the time of year in your chosen destination. It is not always warm in the south!

- Find out what travel offers are available for reaching your destination.

- Reserve your accommodation and tickets as far in advance as you can. If you are going to a small town, the hotels may close out of season, or you may find that a local event means all the hotels are full when you arrive.

- If you are taking your car, or you wish to hire one, make sure you have the appropriate documents with you.

- Buy yourself a good local guidebook so that you can get the most out of your trip. The green Michelin guides cover the whole of France.

• Don't forget to switch out the lights when you leave – and *bon voyage!*

CHECKLIST

1. How do you want to use your leisure time – for rest and relaxation, or for meeting new people?

2. Would the level of your French allow you to really enjoy an all-French group activity?

3. Have you enquired about leisure facilities near to your home?

Regional Directory

One of the principal aims of this book has been to provide a broad outline of French life, albeit written by a Londoner-turned-Parisien. It would be impossible to list all the English and Anglo-French associations and services available in France in the space available. I have therefore tried to indicate the most useful information gathered with the help of the British Consulates-General in France, and others, for each of their consular regions. All information is correct at the time of writing, but may be subject to change according to circumstance.

Networking

Do not be shy of contacting the associations ·mentioned in this section. 'Networking' is important for foreign residents in France, especially when they first arrive. In the more traditional sense it may help your employment prospects. However, networking within your local community will allow you to find the best and most appropriate local services for your needs and those of your family.

Not all regions of France have the same variety of facilities and contact organisations. This section is based upon areas traditionally popular with British residents in France. Do not be dispirited if you do not find listings for the region to which you are moving in this brief guide. Both consulates and local tourist information centres often know of groups which may be of interest to foreign residents and new arrivals.

Nationwide organisations

One organisation which does have branches nationwide which may be able to put you in contact with other English speakers in your region is the **Association France-Grande-Bretagne**, 183 avenue Daumesnil, 75012 Paris. Tel: 01 55 78 71 71. Further details of the association, and of local branches, can be obtained from the national headquarters at this address.

The **ex-servicemen's associations**, the Royal British Legion and

Royal Air Force Association, also have branches across France, in Paris, Lyon, the south and the south west. Contact details can be obtained from the nearest British Consulate-General. A full directory of **Church of England chaplaincies** across France can be obtained from the Gibraltar Diocesan Office, 14 Tufton Street, London SW1P 3QZ.

PARIS AND THE PARIS REGION

Unsurprisingly, the Paris region is the best served of all areas of France for English-speakers. There are currently 63 British or Franco-British associations which are members of the 'umbrella organisation' the **British Community Committee** (BCC). The BCC publishes each year a **Digest** of these associations, giving brief details and contact numbers. These range from sports, to education, to social activities, to support groups, and include all the main British political parties.

The Digest is free from the British Consulate in Paris, and can also be found at places such as the British Institute, and the British churches. Places listed below and marked with an asterisk (*) all have free copies of the Digest available. Copies are also available from the Association France-Grande-Bretagne offices in Paris. There are also details of a free volunteer English-language **education information service** provided by the BCC included in the Digest.

All major national, regional and international newspapers and publications are readily available in Paris. For local information on everything from jobs, to housing, to language schools, to where to go out, the following three publications are vital:

- *France–USA Contacts*, 3 rue Larochelle, 75014 Paris – free across Paris. Known as FUSAC.

- *The Free Voice*, 65 quai d'Orsay, 75007 Paris – free across Paris.

- *Time Out in Pariscope*, 100 rue du Faubourg St Antoine, 75012 Paris (supplement in English with the *Pariscope* magazine) – 3 FF at all newspaper kiosks.

Note: In the addresses listed below, M° = nearest Métro station.

Useful addresses in Paris

Consulates
- The British Consulate-General, 16 bis rue d'Anjou, 75008 Paris.

Tel: 01 44 51 31 00. Open Monday–Friday 09h30–12h30, 14h30–17h00. (*)

- The American Consulate, 2 rue St Florentin, 75001 Paris. Tel: 01 44 96 14 88.

- The Canadian Embassy, 35 ave Montaigne, 75008 Paris. Tel: 01 44 43 29 00.

- The Irish Embassy, 4 rue Rude, 75016 Paris. Tel: 01 44 17 67 00.

Cultural centres
- The British Cultural Centre at The British Council, 11 rue de Constantine, 75007 Paris. M° Invalides. Tel: 01 49 55 73 00. (*)

- The Canadian Cultural Centre, 5 rue de Constantine, 75007 Paris. M° Invalides. Tel: 01 47 05 89 68.

- The Irish Cultural Centre, Collège des Irlandais, 5 rue des Irlandais, 75005 Paris. RER. Luxembourg. Tel: 01 45 35 59 79.

Chambers of Commerce
- The Franco-British Chamber of Commerce & Industry, 31 rue Boissy d'Anglas, 75008 Paris. Tel: 01 53 30 81 30. Fax: 01 53 30 81 35. (*)

- The American Chamber of Commerce in France, 21 avenue George V, 75008 Paris. Tel: 01 40 73 89 90.

- Chambre de Commerce et de l'Industrie de Paris, 27 avenue Friedland, 75008 Paris. Tel: 01 42 89 70 00.

- Details of professional associations of British accountants, electrical engineers and civil engineers can all be found in the BCC Digest. There are also contact details for the Paris branches of The Institute of Management, and The Institute of Directors European Centre in France.

Women's associations
The British & Commonwealth Women's Association. Tel: 01 47 20 50 91. Clubroom and library in central Paris, and regular and varied activities throughout Paris and the suburbs. (*)

For information on the following groups, contact the appropriate national consulates: The Association of American Wives of Europeans (AAWE); the American Women's Group (AWG); the Canadian Women's Group; the South African Women's Association. The Association of Irish Women in France can be contacted at 24 rue de Grenelle, 75007 Paris.

MESSAGE mothers' support group (*)

English-speaking multi-national support group providing contact, activities and information for mothers of young children across the region. Ante-natal and post-natal advice available and details of English-speaking facilities. See BCC Digest for current contact number.

Students, au pairs and young workers

* Centre d'Information de la Jeunesse (CIJ) – 101 quai de Branly, 75015 Paris. Principal youth centre for Paris for information on jobs, accommodation and travel, amongst other services.

* Centre Régional des Oeuvres Universitaires et Scolaires (CROUS) – 39 avenue George-Bernanos, 75005 Paris. Tel: 01 40 51 37 10/ 14. Student information centre principally serving students in Paris at the Sorbonne faculties.

* The Collège Franco-Britannique at the Cité Universitaire – 9B boulevard Jourdan, 75014 Paris. Tel: 01 44 16 24 00. One of 37 international halls of residence making up the Cité Universitaire. Students must be at least third year level in the UK. 50 per cent of rooms are reserved for British students.

* The YWCA-Cardew Club, 7 rue Auguste-Vacquerie, 75116 Paris. Tel: 01 47 20 44 02. M° Etoile and Kléber. Open Thursday–Sunday 19h00–23h00 September–June. Free details sent on request. (*) A social club and resource centre for newly arrived young English-speakers of all nationalities in the 18–30 age range. Clubroom in central Paris offering cheap, central and safe meeting point. Wide variety of activities and information available. A good 'networking' point to make friends and branch out in Paris.

Health

* The Hertford British Hospital/Hôpital Franco-Britannique, 3 rue Barbés, 92300 Levallois-Perret. M° Anatole France. Tel: 01 46 39 22 22. Fax: 01 46 39 22 26. (*) British and French staff available in a conventioné hospital within the French social security system.

- The American Hospital of Paris, 63 boulevard Victor-Hugo, 92202 Neuilly sur Seine. Tel: 01 46 41 27 27. Emergency Number 01 47 47 70 15. N.B. This is a private hospital. The care offered is excellent but expensive. Check consultation prices before using this hospital.

Places of worship/community centres
Most English-language churches act as community centres, and you will find details of many events, services and clubs there.

- Church of England – Central Paris: St George's Anglican Church, 7 rue Auguste-Vacquerie, 75116 Paris. Tel: 01 47 20 22 51. M° Etoile and Kléber. (*) St Michael's English Church, 5 rue D'Aguesseau, 75008 Paris. Tel: 01 47 42 70 88. M° Concorde. (*) In the suburbs, lively churches can be found at Chantilly, Fontainebleau, Maisons-Lafitte and Versailles. (*BCC Digest available via all these churches.)

- American Episcopalian Cathedral, 23 avenue George V, 75008 Paris. Tel: 01 53 23 84 00. M° George V.

- Scots Kirk, 17 rue Bayard, 75008 Paris. Tel: 01 48 78 47 94. M° F. D. Roosevelt. (*)

- St Joseph's RC Church (English-language), 50 ave Hoche, 75008 Paris. Tel: 01 42 27 28 56. M° Etoile.

- The American Church, 65 quai d'Orsay, 75007 Paris. M° Invalides or Alma-Marceau. Tel: 01 40 62 05 00. **This is a major community centre in Paris. Come here for accommodation and job offers on the noticeboard.**

- The main Paris Mosque is at 2 Place Puits de l'Ermite, 75005 Paris. Tel: 01 45 35 97 33. M° Monge.

- The main Paris Synagogue is at 44 rue de la Victoire, 75009 Paris. Tel: 01 45 26 95 36. RER/M° Opéra or Le Peletier.

Language schools
See *FUSAC* and *The Free Voice* for a very wide range. The three most well-known are:

- La Sorbonne – 47 rue des Ecoles, 75005 Paris. Tel: 01 40 26 22 11. M° Cluny-Sorbonne.

- Institut Catholique, 90 rue d'Assas, 75006 Paris. Tel: 01 44 39 52 00. M° Rennes.

- Alliance Française, 101 boulevard Raspail, 75006 Paris. Tel: 01 45 44 38 28. M° Notre-Dame-des-Champs.

Sport
The Standard Athletic Club. Tel: 01 46 26 16 09. Fax: 01 45 07 87 63. (*) A private British sports club on the edge of Paris with excellent facilities (tennis, squash, swimming pools, playing fields). Can also put you in contact with other sporting associations (rugby and cricket) as well as home to its own teams (football, hockey, etc.).

NORTHERN FRANCE (INCLUDING NORMANDY)

Because of its geographical proximity to the UK, northern France is an area popular with British residents. Having been invaded by the Normans in 1066, the British have been busy getting their own back in more recent years in the region of France some have nicknamed 'Lower Kent'. Further towards the east, the opening of the Channel Tunnel near to Calais has led to a second wave of immigration in the northern region of France.

Economically, the region has suffered from the widespread problems which have affected employment opportunities in the French construction and other industries, notably the textile industry. Expanding industries in certain parts of Normandy include pharmaceuticals and telecommunications. The Channel Tunnel has had a positive effect on job creation in the immediate surrounding département, but in general the north has been hard hit by factory closures.

Consulates
The British Consulate-General for Northern France is at 11 square Dutilleul, 59800 Lille. Tel: 03 20 12 82 72. Open 09h00–12h00 and 14h00–17h30. Honorary British Consultates can be found at:

- P&OFerries, 41 Place d'Armes, 62100 Calais. Tel: 03 21 96 33 76.

- Cabinet Barron, 'La Clarté', 88–100 Route de Paris, 62200 Saint-Martin-Boulogne. Tel: 03 21 87 16 80.

- L. Deweulf, Cailleret & Fils, 11 rue des Arbres, BP 1502, 59383 Dunkerque. Tel: 03 28 66 11 98.

The British Community Association in the Northern France district sends out regular newsletters with details of forthcoming events, diary dates, general information and times of church services in English in Lille, Arras, Calais and Boulogne-sur-Mer. To contact the Association, write to the Secretary c/o The British Consulate-General in Lille, at the above address.

Education

- Ecole Active Bilingue Jeannine Manuel, 418 bis rue Albert Bailly, 59700 Marcq-en-Barouel. Tel: 03 20 65 90 50. Fax: 03 20 98 06 41. Fee-paying day and boarding school, five minutes from the centre of Lille, offering secondary education up to the baccalauréat.

- Association des Parents Anglophones de la région de Chantilly (ARPEC) – BP 60302, 60304 Chantilly Cedex. Organises classes in English for special needs of children from English-speaking families in the area based at the collège and lycée in Chantilly. Weekly kindergarten classes available and also an official GCSE examination centre.

Normandy
Normandy falls within the Paris British consular district. Honorary British Consulates in Normandy can be found at:

- 31 boulevard Winston Churchill, Cedex 7013, 76080 Le Havre. Tel: 02 35 53 05 98.

- P&O European Ferries, Gare Maritime Sud, 50104 Cherbourg. Tel: 02 33 88 65 60.

Places of worship
Church of England chaplaincies at Caen. (Tel: 02 31 73 82 93) and Rouen (Tel: 02 35 70 51 63).

The **Association France-Grande-Bretagne** has a very active branch in Caen (39 rue de Chemin Vert, 14000 Caen. Tel: 02 31 73 18 80. Fax: 02 31 73 82 93). An **English-speaking association** has also been formed in the more remote rural area around Coutances, and can be contacted via the tourist office there.

The **Normandy Tourist Board** publishes a useful and detailed guide in English (*Normandy in your Pocket*). They can be contacted at either 14 rue Charles-Corbeau, 27000 Evreux, France, or in the UK at 6 Transon House, Victoria Street, Bristol BS1 6AH.

LYON AND THE RHÔNE-ALPES REGION

Lyon is the second principal city in France. The Rhône valley around Lyon has traditionally been a leading centre of industry, but it has suffered economically like other areas from the decline of industry in France. Grenoble is another major French city, with 400,000 inhabitants in a radius of 15km, including a significant student population, and a very developed computer and research industry.

Useful addresses in Lyon

The **British Consulate-General** is at 24 rue Childebert, 69002 Lyon. Tel: 04 72 77 81 70. M° Bellecour or Cordeliers. Open 09h00–12h30 and 14h00–17h00, Monday–Friday.

Business

• The Franco-British Chamber of Commerce is at 31 rue de Grenette, 69002 Lyon. Tel: 04 78 37 99 51.

• In addition to the usual consular services, the British consulate in Lyon also has a Commercial section which offers assistance and advice on marketing in France.

• Chambre de Commerce et de l'Industrie de Lyon, 9 rue de la Bourse, 69002 Lyon. Tel: 04 78 38 10 10. The Chambre operates an international information service at 16 rue de la République, 69002 Lyon.

Places of worship

• Church of England – services every Sunday at 10h30. Tel: 04 78 59 76 06 for details.

• RC Mass in English – 1st Sunday of the month at Notre-Dame de Fourvière. Tel: 04 78 83 77 98 between 19h00–20h00 for details.

Community associations

The British Consulate in Lyon publishes an excellent and comprehensive free information pack for new arrivals in their consular area, listing 12 associations in and around Lyon. Included amongst these are details of women's associations, an English-speaking mothers-and-toddlers group, and luncheon clubs.

Welcome and information services

- Rhône-Acceuil International, 5 place de la Baleine, 69005 Lyon. Tel: 04 78 50 03. Open Thursday 10h00–13h00 and Tuesday 18h30–20h00. Provides social and information services for new arrivals. Also organises French conversation classes.

- Tourist office (**syndicat d'initiative**), Place Bellecour, 69002 Lyon. Tel: 04 78 42 25 75. Open 09h00–18h00 Monday–Friday, 09h00–17h00 Saturday, 10h00–17h00 Sunday.

- Centre régional d'information jeunesse (CRIJ), 9 quai des Celestins, 69002 Lyon. Tel: 04 72 77 00 66. Open Monday 13h00–19h00, Tuesday–Friday 10h00–19h00, Saturday 10h00–13h00 and 14h00–19h00. Regional youth information centre for information on accommodation, jobs and travel. Also has lists of language courses available.

Language schools

- Alliance Française – 11 rue Pierre Bourdan, 69003 Lyon. Tel: 04 78 95 24 72.

- Université Lyon II – 86 rue Pasteur, 69365 Lyon. Tel: 04 78 69 70 00.

- Check also the list of schools at the CRIJ (see above).

Education

Cité Scolaire Internationale, Section Anglophone, 2 place Montréal, 69361 Lyon Cedex 07. Tel: 04 78 69 60 06. Fax: 04 78 69 60 37. A French secondary school with a private international section in central Lyon – 85 per cent French, 15 per cent British and American.

Useful addresses in Grenoble

Grenoble is within the Lyon consular district. A full list of associations of interest to English-speakers is included in the consular information pack available at the British Consulate.

- Church of England services every Sunday at 10h45 at St Marc's Ecumenical Centre, avenue Malherbe, Grenoble. Tel: 04 76 85 46 07 for further details.

- English International, Grenoble – a monthly luncheon club on the first Friday of every month. Tel: 04 76 40 17 22 for details.

- Open House, Grenoble – an English-speaking cultural association which meets at the Centre des Loisirs Clemenceau, 11 avenue Jean Perrot, 38000 Grenoble.

- A cité scolaire internationale (see above) is planned in the département round Grenoble for 1999. You will need to enquire locally for details when you arrrive.

Useful addresses in the surrounding areas
- Franco-British Club, c/o Maison des Associations, Room 22, 2nd Floor, 4 rue André Malraux, 4200 Saint-Etienne.

- Club d'Anglais, 17 rue de la Paix, 74000 Annecy. Tel: 04 50 45 82 41.

- Grapevine, c/o Maison des Jeunes et de la Culture, 4 rue Vaugelas, 73100 Aix-les-Bains. Tel: 04 79 35 24 35.

- Lycée Internationale, BP 159, 01210 Ferney-Voltaire Cedex. Tel: 04 50 40 82 66. Fax: 04 50 40 80 38. A private section offering the British national curriculum within a French state secondary school. Very close to the Swiss border. 50 per cent reduction in fees for unsubsidised families living in the locality (Pays de Gex).

THE SOUTH OF FRANCE

The climate and countryside of the south of France have long drawn English-speakers to settle there. As a result, there is a very developed network of agencies and support groups to help newcomers to the region. Economically, the region is reasonably stable, although the Bouches-du-Rhône region around Marseille, and the Alpes-Martime district around Nice, are suffering economically much more than the rest of the south.

Generally, one can divide the south into two areas. The eastern area of **Provence** is nearer to Italy, based around Aix-en-Provence, Marseille and Nice, and includes the legendary Côte d'Azur. **Languedoc-Roussillon** covers the western region bordering Spain, based around Nîmes, Montpellier, Narbonne and Perpignan. Between the two regions lies the wild marshes of the **Camargue**, inhabited by flamingoes, wild ponies and the French gypsies (the **Gitanes**).

Consulates
The British Consulate-General in Marseille covers the entire south

of France: 24 avenue du Prado, 13006 Marseilles. Tel: 04 91 15 72 10. Open Monday–Friday 09h00–12h00 and 14h00–17h00. There are also two Honorary British Consulates in Provence:

* Nice – open Tuesday, Wednesday and Thursday, 10h00–12h00. Tel: 04 93 82 32 04.

* Monaco – open Monday–Friday, 09h00–12h00 and 14h30–18h00. Tel: 00 377 93 50 99 66.

The British Consulate in Marseille provides a full free listing of all associations of interest to English-speakers within its consular district. Addresses given below are a selection from the current list.

Places of worship
There are Church of England chaplaincies in the following towns and cities. Call for details of address and service times:

* Marseille – Tel: 04 91 55 57 38

* Nice – Tel: 04 93 87 19 83

* Cannes – Tel: 04 93 94 04 56. Fax: 04 93 94 04 43

* Sophia Antipolis – Tel: 04 92 92 92 83

* Menton – Tel: 04 93 35 77 41

* Monaco – Tel: 00 377 93 30 71 06

* Beaulieu – Tel: 04 93 01 63 46

* St-Raphael – Tel: 04 94 44 05 67

* Services are also held in Vence. Call the church in Nice for details.

Business
* Franco-British Chamber of Commerce & Industry, Bureau 403, 24 avenue du Prado, 13006 Marseille. Tel: 04 91 81 40 74.

* The Nice branch of the Chamber can be contacted on 04 93 62 94 95.

* The Institute of Directors – Tel: 00 377 93 50 96 86 (based in Monaco).

Health

Sunny Bank Hospital, 133 avenue du Petit Juas, 06400 Cannes. Tel: 04 93 06 31 06 (Anglo-American).

Education

- International School of Sophia Antipolis, CIV BP 97, 06902 Sophia Antipolis. Tel: 04 92 96 52 24. Fax: 04 93 65 22 15. E-mail: asieca a riviera.fr. Website: http://www.ibo;org/schools/civ/civ.htm. A private section within a state-run French primary and secondary school, 40 per cent French, 40 per cent English, 10 per cent American and 10 per cent 'rest of the world'.

- A new international lycée is being established at the time of writing at Luynes near Aix-en-Provence. More details will be available from ELSA in the future.

Community associations

- British Association of the Alpes-Maritimes, Holy Trinity Church, 11 rue de la Buffa, 06000 Nice. Tel: 04 93 87 19 83. The association has branches in Cannes, Nice and Menton.

- British Association of Monaco, BP 41, MC 98001 Monaco Cedex. Tel: 00 377 93 50 19 52. Fax: 00 377 93 50 19 62.

- AAGP (Anglo-American Group of Provence), Aix-en-Provence. Tel: 04 42 26 91 84. Publishes a newsletter and also has a library in Aix.

- Association Culturelle Franco-Britannique de Carpentras, 'La Charité', 77 rue Cottier, BP113, 84204 Carpentras Cedex.

Libraries

- AAGP in Aix-en-Provence (see above).

- English American Library, 12 rue de France, 06000 Nice. Open Tuesday–Friday 10h00–11h00 and 15h00–17h00.

- Beaumont English Language Library, Hameau de l'église Beaumont de Ventoux, 84340 Malaucene. Tel: 04 90 65 25 60.

Newspapers

- *Var Village Voice* – Tel: 04 94 04 49 60.

- *The Riviera Reporter* – Tel: 04 93 45 77 19.

Cricket

For those who miss that most quintessential of British pastimes (apart from drinking tea), there are three (!) cricket clubs in Provence. Details available from the British Consulate in Marseille.

Car insurance

Fonds de Garantie Automobiles, 39 Bd Vincent Delpuech, 13255 Marseille. Cedex 06. Tel: 04 91 83 27 27. For problems arising over car insurance disputes or lack of insurance cover (see Chapter 9).

Useful addresses in Languedoc-Rousillon

Honorary British Consulates:

- Montpellier – Tel: 04 67 15 52 07.

- Perpignan – Tel: 04 68 54 92 03.

The British Cultural Association, 4 rue de l'Université, 34000 Montpellier. Tel: 04 67 66 09 08.

Association France-Ecosse, avenue des Moulins, BP 3067, 34034 Montpellier. Cedex 1. Tel: 04 67 79 01 58.

Montpellier Cricket Club, 20 rue Ernest Michel, 34000 Montpellier. Tel: 04 67 58 83 63.

SOUTH-WEST FRANCE

To a large extent, the Dordogne has taken over where Provence left off as a favoured holiday and retirement destination for British residents in France. The two principal – and rival – cities of the region are Bordeaux and Toulouse. Residents of one city will never say anything good about the other city, so do not be put off by any stories they might tell!

Bordeaux has a long association with England through trade and commerce. Toulouse acquired a significant British population with the arrival of the aerospace industry. The city also has a thriving student population at the university. Biarritz, once the favoured resort of the British royal family, is now the surf capital of France. However, it still retains a great deal of elegance. The inner countryside of the Dordogne is the area where you are most likely to find the new British 'colony', many of whom are retired.

Useful addresses in south-west France

Consulates
The British Consulate-General in Bordeaux covers the whole area: 353 boulevard Wilson, 33073 Bordeaux Cedex. Tel: 05 57 22 21 10. Fax: 05 56 08 33 12. Open Monday–Friday 09h30–12h30 and 14h30–17h00. There are two Honorary British Consulates in the region:

* Toulouse – Tel: 05 56 61 15 02 02. Fax: 05 61 15 08 92.

* Biarritz – Tel: 05 59 24 21 40.

Places of worship
There are four Church of England chaplaincies:

* Bordeaux and Aquitaine – Tel/Fax: 05 56 40 05 12. Services are held throughout the region on a 'once a month' basis.

* Toulouse – Tel: 05 61 85 17 67.

* Pau – Tel: 05 59 62 56 45.

* Biarritz – Tel: 05 59 24 71 18.

Business
* Franco-British Business Association Bordeaux South-West – Tel: 05 56 97 93 25.

* British Business Network, Toulouse – c/o AVEC, Immeuble Burolines, 1, 2 bis rue Marcel Dorat, 31700 Blagnac. Tel: 06 89 50 77 76. Fax: 05 63 70 70 41.

Community associations
The British Consulate provides a comprehensive free list of services and associations within its consular district which are of interest to British residents. A list of British-owned establishments (e.g. restaurants, etc.) is also available.

* Bordeaux British Community. N.B. questions related to accommodation and employment are not dealt with by the BBC. Tel: 05 57 64 75 71 for further details.

* Bordeaux-Bristol Association, 13 quai de la Monnaie, 33800 Bordeaux. Tel: 05 56 92 26 21.

* Bordeaux Women's Club – Tel: 05 56 28 08 59.

* Dordogne Ladies' Club – Tel: 05 53 61 11 70.

- Dordogne Organisation of Gentlemen. Tel: 05 53 22 77 95.

- The English Centre – La Girardie, 24400 Les Lèches. Tel: 05 53 80 14 45.

- YES (Your English Society) – 1 rue Pierre Curie, 24000 Périgeux. Tel: 05 53 03 46 38.

- A newsletter in English, 'Anglophones in Aquitaine', is available by calling 05 59 30 47 68.

Educational and library facilities

- The Bordeaux International School, 53 rue de Laseppe, 33000 Bordeaux. Tel: 05 57 87 02 11. Fax: 05 56 79 00 47.

- The British Council, Université Victor Segalen Bordeaux II, Bâtiment L, 3 place de la Victoire, 33076 Bordeaux Cedex. Tel: 05 57 57 19 52.

- Bibliothèque anglaise de l'université, 56 rue du Taur, 31000 Toulouse. Tel: 05 59 61 21 29.

REGIONAL TOURIST OFFICES

If the region you are interested in is not listed in the above selection, try contacting the French Tourist Office in London for details of regional tourist information centres, who may well be able to help you make connections with welcome groups, etc. The numbers listed below are for the Paris offices of each regional tourist office.

	Tel:		Tel:
Auvergne	– 01 44 55 33 33	Lorraine	– 01 44 58 94 00
Aveyron	– 01 42 36 84 63	Lozère	– 01 43 54 26 64
Britanny	– 01 45 38 73 15	Nord-Pas-de-Calais	– 01 48 00 59 62
Franche-Comté	– 01 42 66 26 28	Périgord	– 01 42 60 10 09
Hautes-Alpes	– 01 40 15 04 82	Poitou-Charentes	– 01 44 54 53 00
Hérault	– 01 43 29 86 51	Pyrénées	– 01 42 86 51 86
Limousin	– 01 40 07 04 67	Savoie	– 01 42 61 74 73

Regional reading

Finally, for anybody interested in finding out more about France beyond the **périphérique** (the Paris ring road), an excellent magazine offering full coverage of cultural events and life in the regions of France is *France* magazine (in English). Not only are there regular regional features but also useful holiday contacts throughout France. There are also useful and well-informed articles on current French news. In the UK Tel: (01451) 870871 for further details.

Glossary

Anglophone. English-speaking (normally Anglo-Saxon).
Boucherie. Butcher's shop.
Boulangerie. Baker's shop.
Caisse d'allocations familiales. Local family benefits authority.
Caisse primaire d'assurance maladie (CPAM). Local health authority.
Carte grise. Vehicle registration document.
Chômage. Unemployment.
Contrat de durée déterminée (CDD). Fixed-term contract.
Contrat de durée indéterminée (CDI). Indefinite contract.
Collège. Secondary school (age 11–15).
Commissariat. Local police station.
Déjeuner. (To) lunch.
Dîner. To dine. Dinner.
Epicerie. Grocer's shop.
Fiche d'état civile. Official translation of birth certificate(s) and marriage certificate. Required for numerous official papers including residence permits. Available from your country's consulate or the préfecture or mairie.
Lycée. High school (age 15–18).
Mairie. Town or city hall.
Médecin. Doctor.
Merci. Thank you.
Mutuelle. Complementary health and retirement insurance fund.
Opthalmologiste. 'Optician'. This is the eye doctor who will give you the prescription.
Permis de conduire. Driving licence.
Petit déjeuner. Breakfast. Often abbreviated in slang to petit dej'.
Pharmacie. Chemist's shop.
Préfecture. Police headquarters for a district.
Sapeurs-Pompiers. Fire and ambulance brigade. Often abbreviated to Pompiers.
S'il vous plaît. Please.

Useful Addresses

EMBASSIES AND CONSULATES

The French Embassy, 58 Knightsbridge, London SW7. Tel: (0171) 235 8080.

The French Consulate-General, Visas & Immigration Services, 6a Cromwell Place, London SW7. A French Embassy Web site now also exists.

For details of the British, American, Canadian and Irish consular services in France, refer to the Regional Directory. Within France, look in the *Yellow Pages* (*Pages Jaunes*) for details of other embassies.

L'INSTITUT FRANÇAIS IN LONDON

17 Queensberry Place, London SW7 2DT. Tel: (0171) 838 2144. Tube: South Kensington. Bus: 14, 45a, 49, 70, 74 C1. Open Monday–Friday 10h00–21h30, Saturday 12h00–21h30. Website: http://www.francealacarte.org.uk. E-mail: FranceALC@mail. ambafrance.org.uk.

For anybody seriously considering moving to France, or finding out about the French language, culture or lifestyle, a visit to the French Institute in London is a 'must' if at all possible. The Institute, run by the French government, is at the centre of the French 'village' which has grown up around the adjacent French Consulate and French Lycée in London, opposite the Natural History Museum.

The Institute offers cinema, book and multimedia library, restaurant and language school facilities. Language courses are given at all levels, from beginners to advanced and business courses. Telephone classes are available, as well as classes combined with individual lunchtime sessions. For further details call (0171) 581 2701, fax: (0171) 581 2910 or e-mail: michel.richard@ambafrance. org.uk.

The French newsapers are on free access here, including '*Le Figaro économie*' job section (see Chapter 5 on Employment). A Children's Library is situated in an adjacent building at 32 Harrington Road, London SW7 2DT. Tel: (0171) 838 2144. Not surprisingly, a collection of French shops has grown up around this enclave, where you will have a further selection of reference and fiction books and products.

TRAVEL

French Tourist Office (French Travel Centre), 178 Piccadilly, London W1V 0AL. Tel: 0891 244123 (calls charged at 50p per minute). Fax: (0171) 493 6594. Email: info@mdlf.co.uk Web site: www.franceguide.com/ Or to book holidays on the tour operator site www.fr-holidaystore.co.uk The French Travel Centre is open to visitors Monday – Friday 10h00 – 18h00 and Saturday 10h00 – 17h00. You will find under one roof: an Information Office, Air France (information only), Brittany Ferries, SeaFrance, France Magasin (for maps and guide books), a bureau de change (Bank of Ireland) and the French Holiday Service travel agency.

Student Travel Centre – OTU (Organisme pour le Tourisme Universitaire), 39 avenue Georges-Bernanos, 75005 Paris. Tel: 01 44 41 38 50/40 29 12 12.

Rail Euorpe, 179 Piccadilly. Tube: Green Park or Piccadilly Circus.

Eurostar. Information is available from Waterloo Station, and from all main British Rail and SNCF stations. Paris office: 2 rue de Compiegne, 75010 Paris. Tel: 01 49 70 01 75.

Eurolines Coach Service

For details of destinations not listed, contact one of the offices below:

London: Victoria Coach Station, Buckingham Palace Road, London SW1. Tel: (0171) 730 0202.

Bayonne: 3 place Charles de Gaulle, 64100 Bayonne. Tel: 05 59 59 19 33.

Bordeaux: 32 rue Charles Domercq, 33800 Bordeaux. Tel: 05 56 92 50 42.

Lyon: Gare routière, Centre d'Echanges de Perrache, cours de Verdun, 69002 Lyon. Tel: 04 72 41 09 09. Fax: 04 72 41 72 43.

Paris: 28 avenue Général de Gaulle, 93170 Bagnolet. Tel: 01 49 72 51 51.

Toulouse: 68 boulevard Pierre Semard, 31000 Toulouse. Tel: 05 61 26 40 04.

Vehicle information
French Ministry of Transport. Tel: 01 40 81 21 22/81 87/82 07/82 12.
Automobile Association, PO Box 128, Basingstoke RG21 7XA. Tel:
(01265) 493 750.
Royal Automobile Club, RAC House, PO Box 100, South Croydon
CR2 6XW. Tel: (0181) 686 2525.

BUSINESS CONTACTS

The French Chamber of Commerce and Industry, Knightsbridge
House, 197 Knightsbridge, London SW7 1RD. Tel: (0171) 304
4040. Fax: (0171) 225 5557.
For details of the Franco-British Chambers of Commerce in
Bordeaux, Lyon, Marseille and Paris, and the American
Chamber of Commerce in France, refer to the Regional
Directory. Help can also be obtained from the Commercial
sections of the British Consulates-General in France.
AGIL (Association de Gestion des Intérêts des Libéraux), 9 bis, rue
Montenotte, 75017 Paris. Tel: 01 40 68 78 78. Fax: 01 40 68 78 85.
M° Charles-de-Gaulle-Etoile. An association agréée in central
Paris (see Chapter 5 on Employment) offering full and friendly
advice for those considering establishing themselves in self-
employed activity in France. English spoken.

BANKS

Barclays. The most widely represented British high-street bank in
France, with over 100 branches. Either enquire at your local
branch in the UK for further details; or make an appointment at
your nearest branch when you arrive; or contact the International
Branch, 6 rondpoint des Champs-Elysées, 75008 Paris. Tel: 01 44
95 13 80. Fax: 01 42 25 73 60.
CIC Banque Transatlantique. Part of the newly-privatised nation-
wide CIC banking chain. Provides free basic brochures in English
on French financial issues.
Paris – 17 boulevard Haussmann, 75428 Paris. Cedex 09. Tel: 01
40 22 80 00. Fax: 01 48 24 01 75.
London – 36 St James' Street, London SW1A 1JD. Tel: (0171)
493 6717. Fax: (0171) 495 1018.
Washington DC – 1819 H Street, NW – Suite 620, Washington
DC, 20006. Tel: 202 429 1909. Fax: 202 296 7294.
Citibank. The American bank has a number of branches across

France offering banking services in English. Tel: 01 49 05 49 05. Monday–Saturday 24 hrs a day for further details.

Société Générale. International Private Clients Branch (English-speaking), 29 boulevard Haussmann, 75009 Paris. Tel: 01 53 30 87 10. Fax: 01 53 30 87 30.

EMPLOYMENT AGENCIES

All offices listed are in Paris, but many also deal with clients across France, or may have branches elsewhere in France.

Mainly secretarial

Adecco, 4 place de la Défense, 92090 Paris La Défense. Cedex 26. Fax: 01 46 98 00 08.

Axel, 59 rue des Mathurins, 75008 Paris. Tel: 01 42 66 50 51.

BEPA, 6 rue de Madrid, 75008 Paris. Tel: 01 43 87 48 13.

Femmes & Carrières (Angela Mortimer Group), 21 rue de la Paix, 75002 Paris.

Manpower, 45 avenue Bosquet, 75007 Paris. Tel: 01 45 50 47 12.

Sheila Burgess International, 62 rue St Lazare, 75009 Paris. Tel: 01 44 63 02 57. Fax: 01 44 63 02 59. London office: 4 Cromwell Place, London SW7 2JE. Tel: (0171) 584 6446. Fax: (0171) 584 1824.

TM International, 36/38 rue des Mathurins, 75008 Paris. Tel: 01 47 42 71 00. Fax: 01 47 42 18 87.

Temporary (intérimaire) employment agencies (office/secretarial)

GR Intérim, 12 rue de la Paix, 75002 Paris. Tel: 01 42 61 16 16. Fax: 01 47 03 40 49.

Intérim-Nation. Tel: 01 43 45 50 00/01 42 65 61 26 (temporary and permanent work).

Kelly Girl. Tel: 01 47 47 41 18 (wide variety of positions available).

Minerve Intérim, 422 rue St Honoré, 75008 Paris. Tel: 01 42 61 76 76. Fax: 01 42 60 22 62.

General international employment agencies

Drake Multilingual, 35 rue de la Bienfoisance, 75008 Paris. Tel: 01 42 89 63 63. Fax: 01 42 89 63 40.

Mercuri Urval, 14 bis rue Daru, 75378 Paris. Cedex 08. A very large general French recruitment agency operating across France, dealing mainly with managerial positions. British office: 29

Grove Hill Road, Harrow-on-the-Hill, Middlesex. Tel: (0181) 863 8466. Fax: (0181) 861 1978.

Michael Page, 159 avenue A. Peretti, 92200 Neuilly sur Seine. Tel: 01 41 92 72 72. One of the largest international recruitment agencies, operating in a wide variety of employment areas.

Austin Knight and PA Consulting both have French offices which can be contacted via the British agencies. They also place advertisements regularly in the French press.

Au pair and nanny agencies

Au pairs échange (French agency), 17 Grovewood, Kew, London TW9 3NF. Tel/fax: (0181) 332 9634.

Away. Tel: (Paris) 01 64 23 44 74.

Bloomsbury Bureau, 37 Store Street, London WC1E 7BH. Tel: (0171) 813 4061.

England and Overseas Nanny Bureau, Suites 21–23 Kent House, 87 Regent Street, Piccadilly, London W1R 7HF. Tel: (0171) 494 2929. Fax: (0171) 494 2922.

Euro Employment Centre, 15 Church Lane, Prestwich, Manchester M25 1AN. Tel: (0161) 798 0311. Fax: (0161) 798 8377.

Good Morning Europe, 38 rue Traversière, 75012 Paris. Tel: 01 44 87 01 22. Fax: 01 44 87 01 42.

International Nannies. Tel: (Paris) 01 47 05 41 33. Fax: 01 47 05 41 43.

Nannies Incorporated. Tel: (Paris) 01 45 74 62 74. Fax: 01 45 74 69 71. Tel: (London) (0171) 437 1312.

NAPP. Tel: (Paris) 01 47 64 46 87. Fax: 01 47 64 48 20.

Paris Nannies Soames International. Tel: 01 64 78 37 98 (nannies, maternity nurses, au pairs, mothers' helps).

Transcontinental Staff Agency, 18 High Street, Beckenham, Kent BR3 1BL. Tel: (0181) 650 2344. Fax: (0181) 650 5645.

TAX ISSUES

Inland Revenue, EC Unit, Room S20, West Wing, Somerset House, London WC2R 1LB.

ACCOMMODATION

Enquire locally for details of how and where to look for accommodation. Most large SNCF stations have a hotel accommodation service. Enquire also at local tourist offices (*syndicats*

d'initiative). In Paris, three places may be able to help:
Accueil des Jeunes en France, 119 rue St Martin, 75004 Paris. Tel: 01 42 77 87 80. M° Chatelet.
Union Chrétienne des Jeunes Gens de Paris (YMCA) for those under 26, 14 rue de Trévise, 75009 Paris. Tel: 01 47 70 90 94.
Union Chrétienne des Jeunes Filles (YWCA), 22 rue de Naples, 75008 Paris. Tel: 01 45 22 23 49.

HEALTH AND WELFARE

Details of English-speaking health facilties are included in the Regional Directory. English-language consulates also have lists of local practitioners who provide services in English.
England, Scotland and Wales – The Department of Social Security, Overseas Branch, Newcastle upon Tyne NE98 1YX.
Northern Ireland Social Security Agency, International Services, 24–42 Corporation Street, Belfast BT1 3DP.
Centre des relations internationales, Sécurité Sociale, 175 rue de Bercy, 75586 Paris. Cedex 12. M° Gare de Lyon. Tel: 01 40 19 53 19.

Refer to Chapters 6 and 7 for information relating to particular benefits, and the agencies you should contact in the UK regarding the transferral of any rights. See page 137 for a list of emergency telephone numbers in France.

DISABILITY AND HANDICAP

Information regarding assistance for the disabled is given in Chapters 4, 7 and 9. Travel guides are also available in the UK from:
RADAR, 12 City Forum, 250 City Road, London EC1V 8AF. Tel: (0171) 250 3222.
Tripscope, The Courtyard, Evelyn Road, London W4 5JL. Tel: (0181) 994 9294.
Mobility International, 2 Colombo Street, London SE1 1JX. Tel: (0171) 403 5688.

EDUCATION

The English Language Schools Association, 43 rue des Binelles, 92310 Sèvres. Tel: 01 45 34 04 11. Fax: 01 45 34 76 63. E-mail: Association. Sis@wanadoo.fr. Refer also to the Regional Directory.

The British Council Education Information Service, 10 Spring Gardens, London SW1A 2BN and the Council's Fellowship Section at Medlock Street, Manchester M15 4AA, will be able to provide details of exchange programmes and scholarship opportunities in French higher education establishments.

BOOKSHOPS

The French Bookshop (UK) Ltd, 28 Bute Street, South Kensington, London SW7 3EX. Tel: (0171) 584 2840. Fax: (0171) 823 9259. Just across the road from the Institut Français. Daily French newspapers and magazines available on mail order.
France Magasin, Digbeth Street, Stow-on-the-Wold, Gloucester-shire GL54 1BN.
France Magasin, 29–30 Palace Street, Canterbury, Kent CT1 2D2.
France Magasin, The French Travel Centre, 178 Piccadilly, London W1 (see above).
WH Smith, 248 rue de Rivoli, 75001 Paris. M° Concorde.
Brentano's, 37 avenue de l'Opéra, 75002 Paris. M° Opéra.
Shakespeare & Co, 37 rue Bûcherie, 75005 Paris. M° St-Michel.
Tea & Tattered Pages, 24 rue Mayet, 75006 Paris. M° Duroc.
The Abbey Bookshop, 5 rue de la Parchemenerie, 75005 Paris. M° St Michel.
Bradley's Bookshop, 8 cours d'Albret, 33000 Bordeaux.
Books & Mermaides, 3 rue Mirepoix, 31000 Toulouse.
Chimera, Faubourg St Privat, 46800 Montcuq.

PLACES OF WORSHIP

Refer to the Regional Directory.

Further Reading

GUIDES

The AA Essential Explorer Guide to France, Adam Ruck (AA Publishing, 1995).
France by Train, Simon Vickers (Hodder & Stoughton, 1994).
How to Get a Job in France, Mark Hempshell (How To Books, 1993).
Le 'Challenges' guide du CV, Pierre Sahnoun and Chantal Goldstein (Editions Générales FIRST, 1994).
Living and working in France, David Hampshire (Survival Books, 1996).

There are a wide variety of guides to France for all tastes and budgets. The classic series remains the Michelin guides, for general information, restaurants and hotels.

HISTORY

France & Britain 1900–1940; Entente & Estrangement, Philip Bell (Longman, 1996).
France & Britain 1940–94; The Long Separation, Philip Bell (Longman, 1997).
The Identity of France Vols. 1 & 2, Fernand Braudel (Fontana, 1991).

SOCIAL SECURITY

Social Security Abroad (pamphlet number NI38).
Your Social Security Insurance Benefits & Health Care Rights in the European Community (pamphlet number SA29).

Both pamphlets are available free from the International Sections of the Department of Social Security listed above.
Le Particulier grand dossier: Démarches et Formalités N°909b, April 1998. An indispensable guide to French paperwork from the

cradle to the grave, covering all aspects of life and leisure. Published by the 'Le Particulier' magazine and available at their bookshop, 'La Maison du Particulier', 21 boulevard Montmartre, 75002 Paris. M° Richelieu-Drouot. Open Monday–Friday 09h30–13h00, 14h00–17h30. Tel: 01 40 20 71 91.

BUSINESS

L'Expansion (general business information in France, regular surveys, etc.) – available throughout France. Bookshop at 14 boulevard Possonnière, 75308 Paris. Cedex 09. Subscriptions *abonnements*). Tel: 03 44 12 52 30.

GENERAL

France Magazine. General French lifestyle subscription magazine offering good nationwide coverage and lots of holiday contacts etc. Tel: (01451) 832218 for further details.

Index

GETTING A JOB ABROAD
The handbook for the international job-seeker: where the jobs are, how to get them

Roger Jones

Now in a fifth fully revised edition, this top-selling title is essential for everyone planning to spend a period abroad. 'A highly informative book . . . containing lots of hard information and a first class reference section.' *The Escape Committee Newsletter.* 'An excellent addition to any careers library . . . Compact and realistic . . . There is a wide range of reference addresses covering employment agencies, specialist newspapers, a comprehensive booklist and helpful addresses . . . All readers, whether careers officers, young adults or more mature adults will find use for this book.' *Newscheck* (Careers Services Bulletin). Roger Jones is a specialist writer on expatriate and employment matters.

336pp illus. 1 85703 418 X. 5th edition.

TEACHING ABROAD
How and where to find teaching and lecturing jobs worldwide

Roger Jones

This revised and updated third edition meets a real demand for practical and realistic information. 'Comprehensive and well researched – invaluable.' *Education.* 'Covers all the main aspects of the subject.' *Wanderlust.* 'A wonderful book, reviews teaching opportunities in over 180 countries and includes addresses for the Ministry of Education in each.' *Career Bookstore (Canada Employment Weekly).*

192pp. illus. 1 85073 276 4. 3rd edition.

BACKPACKING ROUND EUROPE
How to explore Europe on a budget

Mark Hempshell

Now it its second updated edition, this practical guide tells you all you need to know including how to plan your trip, how to get bargain-priced travel and accommodation, what to see and do – plus how to get by on £20 a day or even less. 'Includes practical information on travel in Europe, including dealing with emergencies.' *Family Circle.*

128pp. illus. 1 85703 597 6. 2nd edition

SPENDING A YEAR ABROAD
A guide to opportunities for self-development and discovery around the world

Nick Vandome

A year abroad is now very popular among thousands of school leavers, students, and people taking a mid-life break. This book sets out the numerous options available. 'Should be required reading . . . Unlike most reference books this one should be read right through, and that is a pleasure as well as being very informative. It is totally comprehensive . . . very good value for money.' *The School Librarian.* 'Excellent.' *Careers Guidance Today.* Nick Vandome is a freelance writer who has spent a year abroad on three occasions, in France, Australia, Africa and Asia.

176pp illus. 1 85703 544 5. 4th edition.

FINDING VOLUNTARY WORK ABROAD
All the information you need for getting valuable work experience overseas

Mark Hempshell

The updated third edition of this practical handbook helps you check out the skills, qualifications and experience you might need for all kinds of voluntary work, and find out about the variety of opportunities throughout the world.

160pp. illus. 1 85703 496 1. 3rd edition.

GETTING A JOB IN EUROPE
How to find short or long-term employment throughout Europe

Mark Hempshell

Now in its fourth revised edition, this book sets out the range of opportunities that exist in Europe. Relevant to job-hunters of all levels and from any country. It is full of key contacts, sample documents and hard-to-find information, making it the essential starting point for anyone job-hunting in Europe. 'I learned a lot from the book and was impressed by the amount of information it contained.' *Newscheek, Careers Service Bulletin.* Mark Hempshell is a specialist writer on international employment topics. His other books including *Finding Voluntary Work Abroad.*

208pp. illus. 1 85703 535 6. 4th edition.

MANAGING YOUR PERSONAL FINANCES
How to achieve your own financial security, wealth and independence

John Claxton

Start to control your money – instead of letting it control you. This book shows you how to become your own financial advisor. find out how to protect your income, invest surplus funds, reduce your tax bill and develop your own financial strategy. The methods are here, together with lots of sound ideas to help rid you of money worries once and for all. '...includes tips on [how to] avoid debt, finance your retirement, acquire new financial skills, increase your income and much more.' *The Express.* John Claxton is a successful Chartered Management Accountant and Chartered Secretary who also teaches personal finance.

160pp. illus. 1 85703 581 X. 4th edition.

PAYING LESS TAX
How to keep more of your money for saving and investing

John Whiteley

This money-saving book reveals how you can pay less tax – and not just on what you earn. Value added, capital gains, inheritance, and business tax are covered too, with special sections on forming partnerships and limited companies. Discover how to take advantage of allowances, reliefs and exemptions, and avoid interest, penalties and surcharges. Whatever your age or status, this book will have something for you. From timing your transactions so as to reap maximum benefit, to the pros and cons of tax exile. 'Extremely practical and digestible.' *Financial Mail on Sunday.*

144pp. illus. 1 85703 579 8. 2nd edition.

MAKING A WEDDING SPEECH
How to prepare and deliver a confident and memorable address

John Bowden

How do you find the right words for that all important wedding speech? Written by an experienced public speaker, this entertaining book shows you how to put together a simple but effective speech. Whether you are the best man, bridegroom, father of the bride or other speech-giver, you'll find help at all stages from great opening lines to apt quotations, anecdotes, tips on using humour, together with 50 short model speeches which you can use or adapt. 'Invest in a copy...packed with opening lines, jokes and model speeches.' *Brides Magazine*.

166pp. illus. 1 85703 385 X. 4th edition.

PLANNING A WEDDING
A guide to all aspects of preparation

Mary Kilborn

Now in its fourth edition, this indispensable book fills the need for a really practical, step-by-step guide on the whole process of planning a wedding. With useful planners and checklists, it covers: getting engaged, buying the ring, making announcements, wedding ceremonies and marriage vows, organising the reception, speeches, gifts, honeymoon arrangements and more. There is also helpful advice on particular situations such as mixed marriages, how to cope with divorced parents, even how to get married on a beach in the Bahamas

144pp. illus. 1 85703 487 2. 4th edition.

MAKING MONEY FROM LETTING
How to buy, prepare and manage residential property for rent

Moira Stewart

Have you ever thought about investing your money in property? This book is for anyone who has ever considered letting, whether the property already exists or not. You will learn how to buy and prepare property, how to find a tenant, how to run and manage the property, how to decide whether to use a letting agency and when it is appropriate to seek professional advice. In jargon-free language, and in a straightforward way, this book sets out all that prospective landlords need to know to profit from letting, understand taxation and minimise the risk to their investment. Moira Stewart has had many years' experience of letting property and is a successful private landlord.

160pp illus. 1 85703 493 7. 2nd edition.

SECURING A REWARDING RETIREMENT
How to really understand pensions and prepare successfully for your retirement

Norman Toulson

With the erosion of the once dependable welfare state, preparing for retirement is becoming increasingly important. Most people have relatively little knowledge of what pension prospects they and their dependants have, both from National Insurance and from other sources. This book pinpoints the sources available and the opportunities they offer to mould them to fit their circumstances. Whether you are early in your career, about to make a voluntary or enforced job change, or nearing retirement, this book will help you to plan a financially secure future. Norman Toulson has spent more than 30 years mastering the complexities of the world of pensions and has written six books and almost two hundred articles on the subject.

144pp illus. 1 85703 286 1.